THE FIVE PORCHES

REDISCOVERING THE FIVEFOLD

I would like to dedicate this book to my Dad and Mom, Dr. Charlie and Suzy Fowler. Thank you for setting the example for me to follow. You both have served the Lord all of your lives. Dad, since you answered the call to preach at the age of 16, you have been faithful to preach the unadulterated Word of God for over 57 years throughout America and the nations. Mom, from a child with Grandpa and Grandma on the mission field and ministering with Dad all over the world these last 54 years, you too have been faithful.

Thank you for training me up in the way I should go. Thank you for teaching me so many things. Mom, who knew when you were my homeschool teacher and you were teaching me the alphabet with those little paper bag, letter puppets that I would be an author? Just think when I was a teenager, I didn't even like English and had a hard time with grammar. All of your hard work paid off! You're still my favorite Teacher!

Dad, thank you for putting up with all of my questions about the Fivefold after the Lord gave me a vision about them. You even ordered Kenneth E. Hagin's Book, "The Ministry Gifts" and taught a series on the Fivefold.

Dad and Mom thank you for showing me what true love is. Thank you for teaching me to walk uprightly before the Lord. Thank you for modeling before me what it means to be a servant leader. Your constant acts of humility and selflessness have shaped me into the man of God that I am today. Thank you for your lifestyles of prayer and fasting. Thank you for your unwavering faith in God in the midst of seemingly insurmountable odds. No matter what you both have remained faithful. Even in the loss of our home to a house fire, you were resolute. In Plane crashes you were faithful and showed me how to overcome fear and keep flying. Through financial hardships you showed me how to continue to be generous and give our way out of them. Thank you both for keeping on, keeping on. Dad and Mom you are the greatest man and woman that I know and I'm proud to be your son. I love you forever, Joshua

FOREWORD BY DR. BILL HAMON

THE FIVE PORCHES

REDISCOVERING THE FIVEFOLD

Advantage BOOKS

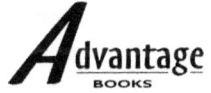

JOSHUA FOWLER

The Five Porches by Dr. Joshua Fowler
Copyright © 2025 by Joshua Fowler
All Rights Reserved.
ISBN: 978-1-59755-814-3

Published by: ADVANTAGE BOOKS™, Orlando, FL, www.advbookstore.com

All Rights Reserved. This book and parts thereof may not be reproduced in any form, stored in a retrieval system or transmitted in any form by any means (electronic, mechanical, photocopy, recording or otherwise) without prior written permission of the author, except as provided by United States of America copyright law.

Unless otherwise noted, scripture quotations are taken from the NEW KING JAMES VERSION®. Copyright© 1982 by Thomas Nelson, Inc. Used by permission. All rights reserved.

Scripture quotations marked (Amp) are taken from the AMPLIFIED® BIBLE, Copyright© 1954, 1958, 1962, 1964, 1965, 1987 by the Lockman Foundation Used by Permission. (www.Lockman.org)

Scripture quotations marked MSG are taken from THE MESSAGE, copyright © 1993, 2002, 2018 by Eugene H. Peterson. Used by permission of NavPress, represented by Tyndale House Publishers. All rights reserved.

Scripture quotations marked (NASB) are taken from the NEW AMERICAN STANDARD BIBLE®, Copyright© 1960, 1962, 1963, 1968, 1971, 1972, 1973, 1975, 1977, 1995 by The Lockman Foundation. Used by permission.

Scriptures quotations taken from the Holy Bible KING JAMES VERSION (KJV), public domain.

Library of Congress Catalog Number: 2025930328

Name:	**Fowler**, Joshua., Author
Title:	***The Five Porches***
	Joshua Fowler
	Advantage Books, 2025
Identifiers:	ISBN Paperback: 978159758143
Subjects:	Books › Religion: Christian Life - Inspirational
	Books › Religion: Church Leadership
	Books › Religion: Adult Education

First Printing: January 2025
24 25 26 27 28 29 30   10 9 8 7 6 5 4 3 2 1

Acknowledgements

To My loving Wife,
Baby, thank you for believing in me and encouraging me through this lengthy writing process. Thank you for dreaming with me. All of our dream drives and long conversations about this book have been so instrumental in it's completion. Anywhere with you is better!
I love you forever and a day!
Joshua

To all of my Children and Grandchildren,
Thank you for continuing the legacy of The Five Porches. When I look at each of you I have hope for the future. I know you will all play very significant roles in the Kingdom of God for many years to come!
I love you to the moon and back and again and again!
Dad aka Opa

To my little Sister, Charm,
Thank you for always having my back and all you do behind the scenes to make the ministry of Awake The World so successful. It's always been you and me. You're my oldest friend. I didn't say you were old. If I said that I would have to be old too! Haha I decided we will just skip old and just renew like the eagles!
I love you more than Chips & Salsa!
Joshua

Mom & Dad Black,
Thank you for giving me the best gift I've received this side of salvation, when you gave me your daughters hand in marriage. Thank you for all you do for our family and ministry. Your tireless and selfless servants hearts are so greatly appreciated.
I love y'all more than we love to braai and eat biltong!
Joshua

Zoë,
Thank you for helping edit this book. You are so amazing, Baby Girl! I'm Papa Proud of you!
Love, Dad

Anna Marques,
Thank you for helping design the book cover! You have an amazing eye.
Love ya, Papa J

To Everyone who calls me Papa!
Those of you who pursue me as spiritual sons and daughters and you know who you are, you are one of the primary reasons this book has been birthed. The demand you place upon His grace and gift in my life, play a tremendous role in helping me to remain reliant upon Him. It is my prayer that you all will help model this in the earth. That you won't be satisfied with the old wineskins of religiosity and the status quo, but you will unpack these truths in your cities, regions and nations. Let us build and establish The Five Porches for future generations to know the fullness of Christ and The Greater Glory that has been promised.
Love & Honor, Papa

Thank you to the following Leaders who've impacted my life: Bishop Bill Hamon, Tom & Jane Hamon, Dutch & Ceci Sheets, Chuck Pierce, RealTalk Kim, Mark & Mary VanGundy, Dana & Nan Gammill, Isaac Pitre, Candice Smithyman, Barry Maracle, David & Nicole Binion, Ron Carpenter, Dr. Rod Parsley, Sammy Rodriguez, Samuel Brassfield, Bill Johnson, Tyrone & Una McFarland, Janet Rae Askins, Barbara Yoder, Ana Werner, Mike & Cindy Jacobs, Patricia King, William & Paula Canfield, Jim & Renee Cutter, Todd & Xio Callahan, Michael & Sandra Scantlebury, Tammy Chism, Ryan & Jennifer Denton, Ricky & Joni Franklin, Kim Clement, Dr. Dan White, N.H. Dutton, Rick Davidson.
Love & Honor, AJ

To all of our Partners,

Thank you for your prayers and support. Your generosity is what makes it possible for me to spend time with the Lord and write books such as this. I decree that you too will have a part in the harvest of souls and the maturity of believers that this book brings in Jesus name.

Love & Honor, AJ

Joshua Fowler

Endorsements

Dr. Joshua Fowler's ***The Five Porches*** is a transformative guide for believers seeking to unlock the fullness of their spiritual calling. Drawing on profound biblical insights and personal revelation, Dr. Fowler reintroduces the significance of the five-fold ministries—apostle, prophet, evangelist, pastor, and teacher—highlighting their essential role in equipping the Church for unity, maturity, and revival.

This is more than a book; it is a call to action for those ready to step into their divine destiny and participate in ushering in sustainable revival. A must-read for anyone longing to see the Church fully equipped and operating in the power and purpose God intended!

Ron Carpenter, Apostle / Author
Redemption Church, San Jose, California

****

I first met Joshua Fowler in the late 90s and, over the years, have witnessed firsthand his unwavering, passionate pursuit of the Lord. Even amid great personal loss, he has remained steadfast to his call - helping usher the nations into awakening, revival, and reformation.

The truths revealed in Joshua's new book, ***The Five Porches - Rediscovering the Fivefold Ministries***, provide prophetic pictures and apostolic blueprints to assist the Ekklesia in forging forward until Christ's return. I highly recommend both the book and the author. They are proven principles from one who bears the marks of a pioneer and has laid down his life so that Christ might receive the fullness of His inheritance. This book is not just an echo of what has been written before; it's a manual for future generations.

Dutch Sheets, Best-selling author
GiveHim15.com, DutchSheets.org

The Five Porches is not just another book—it's a divine blueprint for the Ecclesia God is building in these critical times. Dr. Joshua Fowler masterfully lays out a prophetic revelation of the Fivefold ministries and their role in this last days building project. His prophetic insights, wrapped in personal encounters with Jesus, will stir and awaken you. It's time to stop limiting our ministries to one or two dimensions. The Fivefold anointing must come together, not as competing entities, but as complementary forces of revival, delivering the Church into its finest most glorious chapter of history. ***The Five Porches*** is more than a read; it's an impartation of grace that will transform your ministry and position you to see miracles, signs, and wonders manifest in your life. This is not just a book for pastors or leaders, but for every believer who desires to step into the fullness of Christ's purpose for their lives. The Five Porches is a must-read for anyone who is serious about updating their map for revival and awakening in this generation!

Dr. Lance W. Wallnau, CEO Lance Learning Group
Dallas, TX

****

Dr. Joshua Fowler's book, ***The Five Porches***, is a brilliant reconstruction/reimagining of the scope, role and power of the Fivefold ministries. It is filled with weighty insights from scripture as well as wonderful personal revelations given him by God. This work will assist the people of God in attaining a new vision for the Kingdom of God, as it is brought out of heaven to the earth in the image of Jesus Christ and breath new life into their own alignment with the ways of God. This book is anointed by the Holy Spirit and I know you will feel the presence of the Holy God as you read it. Read it prayerfully and the Holy Spirit will give you a divine impartation of wisdom tailored just for your life.

Joan Hunter, Author/Evangelist
Host of Miracles Happen! TV show

****

I have heard the expression "he is a triple threat", referring to the obvious giftings of an accomplished individual. I regard Dr. Joshua Fowler as a triple threat to the kingdom of darkness and a tried and tested overcomer in the Kingdom of God. Filled with insight, he overflows with wisdom, integrity and life experiences. I have had the opportunity to minister with Dr. Fowler over the past 25 years, and his ability to teach, preach and prophecy, coupled with his humility and time proven biblical experiences make it obvious to me that the anointing of God has been endowed upon him. In his new book *The Five Porches* there is a clear, clarion sound resulting in a fresh understanding and new insight into the Fivefold ministry. Dr. Fowler has skillfully directed his readers to reexamine how the gifts, grace. and government of God apply to the believer. This book is clear, concise and compelling. I encourage each of you to get your copy and revisit this timeless topic with your friends.

Dr. Clarice Fluitt, Prophet, Life Strategist, TV Personality,
Best Selling Author, Motivational Speaker, Entrepreneur

****

I've known Joshua Fowler since the 90s! I had the honor of participating with Bishop Bill Hamon and others when he was commissioned as an apostle and prophet to the nations in 1996. Over the years I've been impressed by his unwavering commitment to the Lord and his heart to see the body of Christ come into the fullness of Christ.

In his book, The Five Porches, Joshua reveals these divine secrets of the Fivefold in a fresh and succinct manner. I love how he interweaves biblical principles together with his personal encounters in the Glory. *The Five Porches*, unveils Kingdom Blueprints for the Ecclesia to come into the greater authority revealed in the New Testament. When we as leaders and believers apply these truths we will be fully equipped and empowered to usher in the Harvest.

Barbara J Yoder, Founding and Overseeing Apostle, Author
Shekinah Christian Church, Ann Arbor, MI

****

It's an "ALL- hands on deck" season we are in. As the warfare has changed, so must the mentality shift -from that of building a single unit ministry, to a broader perspective of a fully functional church . God's bringing a collaboration of powerful and equipped warriors to do severe damage against the enemy's camp. We can't do this alone. It takes everyone coming up to the family table and doing their part. You are a part of the family; it's part of your inheritance. If you have ever wondered- how I really fit into this Fivefold ministry- then this will help bring some clarity. When Dr. Joshua Fowler sent me this book, everything in me jumped for joy and yelled, "YES! HALLELUJAH!" I believe Joshua's book, *The Five Porches,* will help the church shift and adjust to advancing forward. It's time for the Believers of JESUS to step up and Govern for the Kingdom of GOD.

Ana Werner, Founder of Eagles Network
Seer, Prophet, Author, www.anawerner.org

****

The Five Porches is a panoramic view of the Kingdom. This book and Apostle Joshua are both all about the Kingdom of God. *The Five Porches* is not just a Band-Aid coverup to the cancerous problems we are currently dealing with, but through true Biblical principles Joshua prophetically unveils God's original intent and our pathway forward.

Ministering alongside Joshua Fowler is so refreshing, in that he is always living from another place and is always solution oriented. With this book and many of His others, you will find a now word for our world. Just reading *The Five Porches*, you will actually begin to tap into a Spirit of Revelation. So with no reservation, I recommend The Five Porches!. Much love!

Bishop Barry C. Maracle, Founder of TakeCharge Ministries and Transforming U, Best selling author of WAKEUP INTO YOUR Dream

****

Dr. Joshua, your new book on the Fivefold ministries (*The Five Porches*) is powerful. I love the illustrations of the five loaves, five stones and five porches. They are life changing. We need to receive the Fivefold ministries and become Fivefold churches and Fivefold believers to impact our communities, cities and nations of the world!

If we receive this revelation in our lives, we will be changed and set on fire for revival /awakening. That will set the world on fire for Jesus! The four faces of the beings in Ezekiel says they were on fire!
If we will be set on fire with this word and Holy Spirit. There will be no stopping us!

Watch out world, here comes the Fivefold church and believers impacting their world and seeing a multiplication of miracles, souls, finances, resources for the kingdom of God! To GOD be all the glory and praise! Amen!

Dr. Mark VanGundy, RevivalnNations.com
United Kingdom

****

These are unprecedented days of restoration and reformation. God continues to raise up a company of men and women articulating "one sound," with one voice (2 Chronicles 5:13), heralding the glory of the Lord that is filling the earth.

As I read the original first chapter, it is with clarity and simplicity, that *The Five Porches* has accurately and clearly unfolded the Fivefold ministry gifts of Apostles, Prophets, Evangelists, Pastors and Teachers.

God is doing something dramatic and specific in our day and this book imparts powerful insights that help to understand more clearly what the Holy Spirit is doing in the global Church.

In reading the first chapter of this book on *The Five Porches*, I cannot help but consider not only its scholarship but also the experiences and trials, which Joshua Fowler has had, that incubated and sustained the necessity for penning such a book. It is my earnest prayer and expectation that this book will add to your life and be used by the Lord to both, bless and inspire you.

Michael Scantlebury, Apostle, Dominion-Life Int. Min. [dominion-life.org], Author of over 29 published books. apostlemscantlebury.com

I have known Dr. Joshua Fowler since 1992 when he was a student at Valor Christian College. He has traveled the world in fruitful ministry, and he has also seen his share of opposition as he has held true to the faith once delivered to the saints. One thing he has faithfully done during every season of life is to stay positioned to hear what God is saying to the body of Christ in these last days.

In his latest book, *The Five Porches*, Dr. Fowler emphasizes the need to rightly regard the Fivefold ministry office gifts given to the body of Christ. This may seem antiquated in a culture that rejects authority and mocks righteous standards, but it is still a principle that will help lead to success in every endeavor. The men and women who have responded to God's claim on their lives to follow Him into Fivefold ministry have something to say to us. We need to receive them as the gifts they are, and we need to listen to the message they bring. Their words, their lives, and their example will be crucial in leading the church to the victories God has for all of us in the days ahead.

William C. Canfield, Senior Elder
World Harvest Church, Columbus, Ohio

****

I have always admired Dr. Joshua Fowler's heart for legacy and being a spiritual father to many. In this book, ***The Five Porches,*** he ignites an understanding of the Fivefold ministry gifts as a center focus which is missing in the church today. If we want to see the Kingdom of God arise, we need proper instruction and a turning to effective kingdom ministry through activating all of the spiritual gifts that Jesus gave to His church. This book will catapult you into a next level of what we need to become the Fivefold Church for the end times.

Dr. Candice Smithyman, Author, Speaker, Host, Glory Road TV show & Your Path to Destiny. www.candicesmithyman.com

****

Without doubt the Scriptures are very clear that the Five aspects of the fullness of Christ were given as Gifts to the Body of Christ to bring to spiritual maturity His Corporate Body called The Church. Without these five gifts namely the apostle, prophet, evangelist, pastor and teacher there is no true foundation of the Church that Jesus said He would build.

Ephesians 2:20,21 establishes the true foundation upon Christ the Chief Cornerstone. *"You are built upon the foundation of the apostles and prophets with Christ Himself the Chief Cornerstone. IN Him the whole structure is joined (bound, welded) together harmoniously, and it continues to rise(grow, increase) into a holy temple IN the Lord (a sanctuary dedicated, consecrated, and sacred to the presence of the Lord".*

This is the eternal plan for us to become a fixed dwelling place of God in and through The Holy Spirit. We must see the restoration of all five of these gifts in order for everything both in heaven and the earth to be unified and headed up and consummated in Christ. The apostolic fathers joining with the prophetic voices are to send the prophetic evangelists into the very over ripened harvest fields of the nations. Then appoint shepherds not hirelings who will feed the flock and disciple them to go into the marketplaces of the world with the image of Christ to reap this last final great harvest of souls before the soon return of the King of Glory!

Joshua Fowler has laid out the New Testament Pattern of the True Church that must once again represent the fullness of Christ. Christ in us our hope of Glory!

Samuel Brassfield, President, Harvest International Ministries,
Bertram, Texas

****

For such a time as this! That's what I hear the Spirit saying concerning Joshua Fowler's new book *The Five Porches.* What would happen if the body of Christ would truly connect with every joint supplying? The answer is, the church would be revealed in all of its Glory! This is a clarion call for all Fivefold ministers to come together and take the church from division into perfection!

Isaac Pitre, Apostle / Author of The Ascension Dimension,
Dallas, Texas

I am so happy Joshua Fowler wrote this book "**The Five Porches**". Too often we overcomplicate things like hearing God's voice and being led by Him, leaving us confused and doubting, instead of moving forward into all that He has for us. In this practical guidebook, Joshua Fowler gives us the tools we need to keep God the main thing. To stay focused on keeping Him the center of it all so we can walk in even a deeper relationship with Him.

Kimberly Jones, Founder & CEO, Conquering Hell in High Heels
www.RealTalkKim.com

The Five Porches

Foreword by Dr. Bill Hamon

I have known Dr. Joshua Fowler for many years. I performed the dedication service for his baby twin girls who are now grown. Joshua and his family also attended my 70/90 celebration at our 37th annual CI Prophets and Apostles Conference. The conference was celebrating my 70 years of ministry and 90 years of life. Years ago, Joshua traveled with me to Taiwan. He helped me prophesy over numerous people.

Every generation needs to be challenged and activated into the present truth. Dr. Joshua Fowler has been raised up to emphasize the power and purpose of the five-fold ministers. Jesus Christ was and is all five in one person. But the ministers of His Church have received one or more of Christ's attributes of the five-fold ministers of Apostles, Prophets, Evangelist, Pastor and Teacher. Eph. 4:11

The Bible says that Jesus was given the Holy Spirit without measure, but the members of the corporate body of Christ were given one or more of the gifts of the Holy Spirit and a certain measure of grace and faith. I Cor. 12:7-11, Romans 12:3

When Jesus gave the five-fold ministries to the Church, He did not give them to individuals just to make them great ministries with impressive manifestations. No, God gave these ministries to certain of His sons and daughters for one major purpose, for the perfecting/equipping of the saints in their membership ministry in the Body of Christ. For most of my 70 years of ministry I have challenged fellow five-fold ministers to make equipping members of the Body of Christ their priority. The purpose being so that Christ will have a full functioning body enabling Him to fulfill all of His end-time purpose for His corporate body, the Church to fulfill. Eph 4:11-16

Why is the five-fold minister so essential to God? For you who do not know Church history you need to realize prior to 1948 no preacher preached five-fold ministers. They only believed three were active in the

Church prior to 1948, 99% of the Church world did not believe that there were Apostles and Prophets still active in the Church.

One of my main goals during the last 50 years of my ministry has been to make the Prophets and Apostles recognized, accepted and as active in the church as the Evangelist, Pastor and Teacher. I have been functioning as a Prophet since 1954 and God added the Apostolic in 1998.

I thank God for ministers like Joshua Fowler who have been raised up to champion the truth of the five-fold ministers of Christ to His Church. According to Eph 4:13 the five-fold ministers must function until the Church reaches the fulness of the maturity of Christ. It will require the Church to be that in order to fulfill the great move of God that is destined to take place before Jesus 'return.

Thank you Joshua for making this truth available to the Body of Christ.

Bishop Bill Hamon
Bishop: Christian International Apostolic-Global Network
Author: The Eternal Church, Prophets & Personal Prophecy, Prophets & the Prophetic Movement, Prophets, Pitfalls, & Principles, Apostles/Prophets & the Coming Moves of God, The Day of the Saints, Who Am I & Why Am I Here, The Final Reformation & Great Awaking, 70 Reasons for Speaking in Tongues, and How Can These Things Be? God's Weapons of War, Your Highest Calling

Table of Contents

ACKNOWLEDGEMENTS 5
ENDORSEMENTS 9
FOREWORD BY DR. BILL HAMON 17
INTRODUCTION 21
1: A DIVINE ENCOUNTER AND THE FIVEFOLD 25
2: MY PERSONAL JOURNEY 27
3: GIFT CENTRIC VS. CHRIST CENTRIC 31
4: THE FIVE FACETS OF CHRIST 35
5: THE FIVE LOAVES 39
6: THE FIVE STONES 43
7: THE HAND - THE FIVE FINGERS OF GOD 47
8: THE FIVE G'S 51
9: THE FIVE PORCHES 61
10: THE APOSTLE'S PORCH 65
11: THE PROPHET'S PORCH 85
12: THE EVANGELIST'S PORCH 99
13: THE PASTOR'S PORCH 109
14: THE TEACHER'S PORCH 121
15: FIVEFOLD LEADERS, BELIEVERS & CENTERS 131
16: CLEAR VISION 135
17: GET ON THE PORCH! 139
AUTHOR INFORMATION 141

Joshua Fowler

The Five Porches

Introduction

For thus says the LORD of hosts: Once more (it is a little while) I will shake heaven and earth, the sea and dry land; and I will shake all nations, and they shall come to the Desire of All Nations, and I will fill this temple with glory, 'says the LORD of hosts. The silver is Mine, and the gold is Mine, 'says the LORD of hosts. The glory of this latter temple shall be greater than the former, 'says the LORD of hosts. 'And in this place I will give peace, 'says the LORD of hosts. Haggai 2:6-9

In 1989, I had a supernatural encounter with the Lord where I received a vision from the Lord that is etched in my heart to this very day. The Lord showed me a large colosseum packed with people inside and people standing outside wanting to get in. I was standing on the platform speaking and behind me on both sides were several leaders from many states and nations. As I ministered the glory began to fill the room in a tangible way. I could literally see a cloud over the people. The atmosphere was so electrified with the supernatural power of God that you could cut it with a knife. You could smell it like dew or rain. You could taste it like refreshing water. You could hear it like the wind blowing through the trees. The floors reverberated with the Glory of God. I trembled and shook inside as I stood before the Lord in awe. Suddenly I began to see what I couldn't see before, and hear what I couldn't hear before and know what I didn't know before. I began to see with the eye of the spirit beyond the natural realm. I began receiving words of wisdom and words of knowledge and calling out people saying you over here sitting in seat number 1492 stand up and then I proceeded giving them the Word of the Lord. Healings, miracles, signs and wonders were manifesting all throughout the room. Then the Lord would place His hand on my shoulder as if to tell me to wait and I would wait then one of the other leaders from behind me would step out and begin flowing in the Gifts of the Spirit. After he or she ministered they would sit back down, and I would continue speaking or flowing in the

Gifts. Then it would happen again, The Lord would place his hand upon my shoulder and would wait and another leader would step out and begin flowing. I could hear what they were hearing and see what they were seeing as they ministered. One particular time one of these leaders stepped up and began prophetically speaking healing to hearts. He said, "Heart be mended" and all over the room people's hearts were miraculously healed. Broken hearts, people who were bound in the past and even people who had heart disease were healed. I could see what he saw. I saw a green glowing light on each of their hearts as they were being healed. I was blown away. What no counselor or physician was able to heal was healed in this Greater Glory in an instant. As I watched from above with the Lord as we continued ministering below, I asked the Lord who these leaders were and He said, "these are my hands, my Fivefold leaders. I'm bringing my Right and Left Hands together to gather my Harvest and release my Glory in the earth." When I would finish ministering five leaders would walk down both the left and right isles from the platform to the back of the room and Glory would flow so mightily that people were healed and slain in the Spirit as we passed by without touching them. As we walked I remember looking and seeing many people in wheelchairs who even fell to the floor crying. At first I went to pick one up only to find that they were crying tears of joy, because they were healed. I saw legs growing where they weren't before and many other notable miracles. Many who couldn't walk, began walking and praising God.

This vision repeated itself numerous times in different stadiums and arenas in various cities, states and nations throughout the world. We went on two planes from city to city with these Fivefold Teams. We also brought along many other interns and students that we were training and they would go throughout the cities releasing the Glory of the Lord with signs following.

You might be asking, Joshua what does this have to do with the price of tea in China? Well, everything. You see many have prophesied of this Greater Glory for years? Many have saw a great revival and awakening coming for years. Many have received visions and dreams of the greatest harvest of all times. Many have fasted, prayed, sowed with tears and have yet to see this Greater Glory. Many great leaders have come and gone and never saw it's fulfillment. Many revivals and gatherings start out in the Glory, but for some reason it hasn't been sustainable. Many wonder why? I believe as you read on you will discover answers to these and more questions. I truly believe the truths that are uncovered in The Five Porches are essential for us to move from delay to demonstration and frustration to fullness. Yes, The Greater Glory is in sight, it's at hand. Let's GO!

Joshua Fowler

1

A Divine Encounter and the Fivefold

In 1988, I had a supernatural encounter with the Lord. In a vision, I was suspended above the sea with Jesus. Millions of heads were bobbing in the water. He told me they represented the sea of lost humanity.

I saw several tugboats that represented ministries, with John boats and life preservers connected to them, which represented their followers. Jesus asked me, "Why won't they come together?" I replied, "I don't know."

Jesus said these ministries were building man-made kingdoms, not His kingdom. Then James 5:16 rolled across the horizon. Jesus said, "If they would only come together and confess their faults, they would be healed." He dipped His hand beneath the sea and began pulling the plugs. One by one, the tugboats began to sink. Many who were following these ministries sank beneath the sea of lost humanity, while others were barely holding on to boards from the shipwreck.

As the fog rolled away, I saw an aircraft carrier with five planes on the deck. Jesus explained this Spirit-filled aircraft carrier was His ministry, and He was giving me and several others stewardship over it. He told me the planes represented the Fivefold ministries and told me to study them, as I was called to bring them together, raise them, and send them forth.

Jesus then told me the control tower represented divine order and government, which He was bringing back to His church. As we stood, watching, several planes landed and then took off. When a plane landed, those aboard the aircraft carrier would rejoice at the testimonies of the successful missions. They would then refuel the planes with the Word, prayer, and resources before launching them again. There were also rescue helicopters landing on the deck with people they rescued from the treacherous waters of sin.

Since that day the Lord has continued Giving me more insight and understanding about the Spirit-filled aircraft carrier and my mandate to raise up, gather, and commission Fivefold ministers and believers into their destinies.

Let's launch into the Fivefold, exploring how the gifts, the grace, and the government of God apply to us as believers! The enemy has tried throughout the years to stop the church by limiting it to one or two facets of Christ. At best, the church has only functioned with one or two dimensions of the Fivefold. Most churches have a pastor. Some ministries are either teaching centers or evangelical centers. Occasionally, you might find a church that is a prophetic center or an apostolic center. However, most of the time, you will not find a church with all five of the Fivefold ministries functioning together as a Fivefold center

I have had the honor of being sent by the Lord to minister in 37 nations over the last 37 years, and I've seen very few churches functioning in the fullness of the Fivefold anointing. They might reference the Fivefold, except they have not raised up the Fivefold from within their congregation. You may ask, "Why is this important?" It's because Jesus gave these gifts to the church for the maturity of every believer. It's also important because this is the only way we will usher in the Greater Glory into the earth.

2

My Personal Journey

I grew up Pentecostal, specifically in an Assembly of God church, where my great-grandfather was a preacher for 70 years. He went to be with the Lord in 2001. He started out with Dr. Lester Sumrall. Before he joined the Assembly of God, he was a Methodist, although after being filled with the Holy Ghost, he began hanging out with people like Dr. Sumrall, doing tent revivals, brush arbors, and ministering. So, my heritage is rich and deep. My great-grandfather preached for 70 years and was a pioneer in the Assemblies of God. He planted eight churches and because of him, our family became deeply rooted in the Assemblies of God. My dad, Dr. Charlie Fowler has been an ordained Assemblies of God minister for over 57 years.

I grew up in the Assemblies of God church and had never heard about the Fivefold ministries. I understood that if you were called into ministry you were either a pastor or an evangelist. Occasionally, missionaries, who honestly scared me, would come through, and I'd duck, praying, "Lord, please don't send me to another nation. I don't want to eat monkey brains." Evangelists would come in and sometimes they would move in the gifts, and in our church, there would occasionally be a tongue and interpretation. Someone would speak in tongues on one side of the room, and then someone else would give the interpretation. As a kid, I was always puzzled by that. How did they get all that from that? It's amazing how God can share so much through a tongue and interpretation.

But prophecy wasn't the norm. Nobody just stood up and said, "I have a word." I wasn't raised like that. The things we're seeing today weren't the norm for most of the church back then. Prior to the Latter Rain Movement, most of the church didn't understand flowing in different gifts. It was usually just a tongue and interpretation of tongues, people tarrying at the altar, getting filled with the Holy Spirit. However prophets, let alone prophecy, were just unheard of. Someone standing up saying, "I have a word" or "I see a vision" or "The Lord says" — it just didn't happen.

The church has progressed, though, God has been moving the church through phases of accelerated restoration over the last 100 years. Within just the last century, we've witnessed a recovery of the Fivefold ministries. If you look through church history, you'll see it wasn't long ago pastors weren't even called pastors. They were reverends or ministers, and as time progressed, pastors began to be restored. Healing evangelists began to emerge in the '40s, and the term "evangelist" became more recognized. Before that, you didn't see it as much. Pastors began to rise in the '60s, and in the '70s, great teachers like Kenneth Hagin and Kenneth Copeland, Charles Capps, Jerry Savelle, and others began to emerge. These were different leaders God raised up, although before that, the only teachers we knew were schoolteachers or Sunday schoolteachers. The idea of a teacher as a ministry gift, itinerating or being part of a church to teach the Word of God, was new. We only knew evangelists and pastors.

Then, in the '80s, we saw the restoration of prophets — prophets nobody really knew or understood. If you go back to the Latter Rain Movement, you'll see the beginnings of this, except the larger part of the body of Christ didn't receive it. In the '80s, people like Dr. Bill Hamon began to rise, bringing forth the prophetic. In fact, in 1988, at Christian International, God did something significant in their midst, and there was a birthing of the restoration of the ministry gift of prophet. Since then, they've trained hundreds of thousands of prophets around the world.

In the late '90s, we began to see a recovery and restoration of the ministry gift of apostle. The enemy tried to steal these gifts from the church, to keep the church from maturing and fulfilling her assignment. There was an attack on the body of Christ to rob the church of the truth of God's Word. If you go back in history, you'll see a period called the Dark Ages, where they hid the gospel from common believers, only allowing clergy, who were trained in Latin, to understand it. People bled and died so we could

2: My Personal Journey

have the Bible in our own language. How many are thankful for the Word of God?

The Bible says, *"My people are destroyed for lack of knowledge!"* There was an attack on the church and the kingdom to rob us of the truth, the Fivefold ministries, the gifts of the Spirit, and the teachings the early church had. But how many are thankful we're in a time of restoration? Now, you and I can read the Bible for ourselves. We can study to show ourselves approved. We can be like the Bereans and search the scriptures to see if these things are so. But just a few hundred years ago, they couldn't do that. Aren't you thankful you're alive today? Some people laid down their lives, martyred so we could have the truth.

What I'm going to share with you in the next few minutes, I believe, are jewels — principles more priceless than silver, gold, or rubies. These principles, I believe, will help mature the church so we can see the Lord's return. How many want to see the Lord's return? The Bible says He's held up until there's a restoration of all things. So, this is part of that restoration today. We're going to look at the Book. Is that alright? I had a black, minister friend from Pontiac, Michigan who we called Dad Samples and he would say, "Let's take a look at the Book." He was a teacher-prophet, and I'd bring him in to teach. He loved grouper fish, so I'd feed him grouper for breakfast, lunch, and dinner, sitting at his feet, learning from him.

I was 15 years old when a prophet named N.H. Dutton came into my life and prophesied over me, saying, "You'll be a young man with gray hair, and you'll stand before many. My son, take the low road and give me all the glory." He went on to prophesy to me many more things that have come to pass. We never heard of a prophet, yet this prophet came and prophesied things only my dad knew and said specific things that would happen within 90 days, and they did. So, my dad built a room for him — a prophet's quarters. That's how God began to teach me. He brought people like this prophet and others into my life, and I'm so thankful for them. I honor them today as men of God that God used in my life.

> *And He gave some to be apostles, some prophets, some evangelists, and some pastors and teachers. Doing this for to equip the saints for the work of ministry, for the edifying of the body of Christ." I'm thankful we're equipped today. "For the work of ministry, for the edifying of the body of Christ, till we come to the unity of the faith and of the knowledge of the Son of God, to a perfect man. To the measure of the stature of the fullness of Christ. That we should no longer be children, tossed to and fro. Nor carried about with every wind of doctrine, by the trickery of men, in the cunning craftiness of deceitful plotting. But speaking the truth in love. Growing in all things into Him. He who is the head—Christ. From whom the whole body, joined and knit together by what every joint supplies, according to the effective working by which every part does its share. Causing growth of the body for the edifying of itself in love. Ephesians 4:11-16*

The Fivefold ministries bring growth, maturity, and edification to our lives. Some people want to wait until they die to experience heaven, as for me, I want to see heaven on earth. The Greater Glory that so many have prophesied about is waiting for a generation to come together in divine alignment with the Fivefold. Jesus gave us apostles, prophets, evangelists, pastors, and teachers. Jesus gave us these gifts and so we should receive them.

A Foreshadow of the The Fivefold!

> *Now take Aaron your brother, and his sons with him, from among the children of Israel, that he may minister to Me as priest, Aaron and Aaron's sons. Exodus 28:1*

We see a foreshadow of the Fivefold with Aaron and His four sons in this passage. The Old Testament is the New Testament concealed, and the New Testament is the Old Testament revealed. When God established ministry for the first time, He set up a high priest and four sons, symbolizing the Fivefold ministries.

3

Gift Centric vs. Christ Centric

Too many churches are gift-centric rather than Christ-centric. They gather around one gift instead of allowing all Fivefold ministry gifts to work and flow together. Some churches and organizations have reduced every other ministry gift, leading to imbalance. In many of these ministries there's no apostolic ministry, no prophetic ministry, no evangelism, no shepherding, and no teaching ministry.

> *Now this, 'He ascended'—what does it mean other than He also first descended into the lower parts of the earth? He who descended is also the One who ascended far above all the heavens, that He might fill all things. And He gave some to be apostles, some prophets, some evangelists, and some pastors and teachers. They were chosen to equip the saints. Equipping them for the work of ministry. For the edifying of the body of Christ, till we come to the unity of the faith and of the knowledge of the Son of God, to a perfect man. To the measure of the stature of the fullness of Christ; that we should no longer be children, tossed to and fro and carried about with every wind of doctrine. Nor by the trickery of men, in the cunning craftiness of deceitful plotting. But speaking the truth in love. They may grow up in all things into Him who is the head. Christ, from whom the whole body, joined together by what every joint supplies. In accordance with the effective working by which every part does its share, causes growth of the body for the edifying of itself in love. Ephesians 4:9-16*

When is this "till"? "Till we come to the unity of the faith and of the knowledge of the Son of God, to a perfect man, to the measure of the stature of the fullness of Christ." If we lack the Fivefold ministries, we will be unable to be perfected and matured. If we lack the Fivefold ministries, we will not be fully equipped to release the God-intended fire of revival in our spheres of influence. Jesus descended into hell when He was crucified, and when He rose on the third day, He gave these five gifts to the church. He knows this is what the church needs to grow, mature, and work exactly as God has ordained us to be.

Some churches only have a distinctive of one particular gift. They will only listen to a prophet, to a teacher, or to a pastor. Many do not have all five functioning, growing, and flowing in the local Ecclesia. I've visited churches with strong apostles, but no prophets. A prophet only comes to the church as a guest speaker. He might have the time to minister to three or four people, maybe even 100 people. However, the rest of the people never get to partake in personal prophetic ministry. Some say we don't need prophets. I've been to churches with as many as 14,000 members preaching and teaching, but no prophets. They are "non-prophet" organizations. I've been to other churches and conferences where the emphasis is entirely on the prophetic. Everybody's a prophet. I'm a prophet. You're a prophet. Wouldn't you like to be a prophet, too? Everyone is a prophet, and if you're not a prophet, you're not cool. The emphasis on the prophetic is so high the other gifts are devalued.

Many of us naturally function most of our lives in whatever persuasion or church we went to. I'm thankful for the fundamental truths I received from my church. I'm thankful I was saved, sanctified, and filled with the Holy Ghost. I'm thankful for my heritage, only I was never taught about apostles or prophets. In fact, when I finally learned about apostles and prophet, I was told that you could not call yourself an apostle or prophet. If you do, you're lost in pride. The same people take the title pastor from the same list of ministry gifts, and they're fine with that, but they can't go by apostle or prophet.

You might ask, "What does this mean to me? What does this mean for my finances? What does this mean for my marriage? What does this mean for my relationships?" Remember in Ephesians 4 the Fivefold ministries were given as gifts "for the equipping of the saints." When you are fully equipped, your finances will flourish. When you are fully equipped, your

3: Gift Centric vs. Christ Centric

marriage will soar. When you are fully equipped, your relationships will be blessed and fulfilled.

Do you want the fullness of Christ? God will not give the fullness of Christ to babes. No parent would give the keys to their car to a toddler. Many tried and failed when they've given the keys of the Church to immature leadership and immature spiritual sons and daughters. It is essential that leaders and believers commit themselves to being fully equipped.

God wants you to be thoroughly equipped. A house without furniture isn't reaching its full potential, is it? Imagine you invite a family from church to your home, except there's no table to sit at and no dishes for the food. God wishes when people come to your house to learn from you, they receive all facets of the Fivefold ministries. We often sing the lyrics from a song called *Shekinah Glory*, "Release the fullness of Your spirit. Shekinah glory, come. Shekinah glory, come." The fullness of Jesus will not be made manifest simply because we sing or pray for it. It will be made manifest when we receive Jesus as Apostle, Jesus as Prophet, Jesus as Evangelist, Jesus as Pastor, and Jesus as Teacher. He designed it this way.

Joshua Fowler

4

The Five Facets of Christ

Just as a Diamond has many facets, Christ revealed himself through the five facets of the Fivefold that He gave.

As for the likeness of their faces, each had the face of a man. And each of the four had the face of a lion on the right side, the face of an ox on the left side, and each of the face of an eagle. Thus were their faces. Their wings stretched upward; two wings of each one touched one another, and two covered their bodies. And each one went straightforward; they went wherever the spirit wanted to go, and they did not turn when they went. As for the likeness of the living creatures, their appearance was like burning coals of fire, like the appearance of torches going back and forth among the living creatures. The fire was bright, and out of the fire went lightning. And the living creatures ran back and forth, in appearance like a flash of lightning. Now as I looked at the living creatures, behold, a wheel was on the earth beside each living creature with its four faces. The appearance of the wheels and their workings was like the color of beryl, and all four had the same likeness. The appearance of their workings was, as it were, a wheel in the middle of a wheel. When they moved, they went toward any one of four directions; they did not turn aside when they went. Ezekiel 1:10-17

Before the throne there was a sea of glass, like crystal. And amid the throne, and around the throne, were four living creatures full of eyes in front and in back. The first living creature was like a lion, the second living creature like a calf, the third living creature had a face like a man, and the fourth living creature was like a flying eagle. The four living creatures, each having six wings, were full of eyes around and within. And they do not rest day or night, saying:

> *"Holy, holy, holy, Lord God Almighty, Who was and is and is to come! Revelation 4:6-8*

This is a prophetic picture of the face of Christ reflected in the earth through these four faces of these beasts around the throne. You might ask, "Why are there four?"

> *And He Himself gave some to be apostles, some prophets, some evangelists, and some pastors and teachers. Ephesians 4:11*

Do you see how it says "pastors and teachers" together? This is because all pastors must be teachers, nevertheless not all teachers are pastors. This is why they represent the man to the body of Christ. The face of a man first represents pastors caring for the flock. Second, the face of the man represents teachers discipling the body of Christ. The face of the ox represents the evangelist going for the harvest. The face of the eagle represents the prophets soaring into the heavens to see what God has to say, releasing it to the church. The face of the lion represents the apostles uniting the body to take dominion in cities and nations. The apostle's purpose is to deploy the troops to bring in the harvest and fulfill the great commission.

You may be reading this, feeling you are called to represent the face of the lion (the apostle). You may feel you are called to represent the face of the eagle (the prophet). You are the air force of God. God sent you to ascend into the heavens. You may feel you are called to represent the face of the ox (evangelist). God has called you to labor for the harvest as an evangelist. You may feel you are called to represent the face of the man (the pastor and teacher). You are to represent man to God. You have the face of a man, a pastor, or a teacher. You need to know who you are. When you know your identity, you can fulfill your destiny.

Imagine twenty people in a military troop lined up in five rows. This prophetic illustration represents the many facets of the Fivefold anointings flowing together. Let's say the row facing forward represents the pastor. Now, the group turns right face. Now, we have the face of an evangelist paving the way. Right face. Now, we have the face of a teacher. Right face. Now, we have the face of a prophet. Right face. Now, we have the face of an apostle. This is an example of how the Fivefold can flow together to bring in the harvest.

In a season when God says, "It's time for the evangelist to lead the way as we put in the sickle to gather a harvest." The entire church will begin to function with the evangelistic anointing. The church then turns right face. Now, the church is in the prophetic season. The church is then advancing with prophetic precision. Right face. The church then steps into teaching season. It is time to disciple those the church has brought into the kingdom. Right face. Now, it is time to shepherd them. Right face. Now, it is time to send them as arrows to the nations. When the church has the full Fivefold, we can thoroughly equip believers and send them out to fulfill their destiny.

Joshua Fowler

5

The Five Loaves

But He said to them, "How many loaves do you have? Go and see." And when they found out they said, "Five, and two fish." Then He commanded them to make them all sit down in groups on the green grass. So they sat down in ranks, in hundreds and in fifties. And when He had taken the five loaves and the two fish, He looked up to heaven, blessed and broke the loaves, and gave them to His disciples to set before them; and the two fish He divided among them all. Mark 6:38-43

In Mark 6, we see a miracle where Jesus blesses five loaves and two fish from a little boy. The little boy who carried this packed lunch was between the ages of four and six years old. Some might envision the loaves as large, however they were less than a two-piece fish dinner. The Greek translation reveals the "loaves" were five little, cracker-like, thin pieces of bread and two small fish. In fact, one translation describes them as minnows. You might be thinking, "Why mention this?" Through this miracle, God is showing us He wishes to release a multiplication for the body of Christ through the Fivefold!

Jesus came on the scene telling the disciples to sit the people in groups of fifty and one hundred on a grassy area. The Bible says, "He took the bread, He lifted it up, giving thanks. He broke it, He blessed it, and He gave it." Jesus is saying to us today, "Now you go and give it away!" This is how the Fivefold anointing is released.

Have you ever asked yourself where the miracle began? Was it when the boy brought the loaves and fish to Jesus? Was it when Jesus lifted it? Was it when He blessed it and broke it? Was it when He gave it? Was it when the disciples began to distribute it?

I would like to propose to you the miracle began after Christ blessed it, gave it to the disciples, and they began to distribute it to the people. Some think He did this once. I believe He kept breaking it, blessing it, and giving it. When the disciples began to give it away, a multiplication anointing came, and the fire began to spread through the land. Unfortunately, today many believers in churches sit under the Fivefold anointing, only they keep it for themselves. Do you long for miracles, signs, and wonders? Don't keep the anointing to yourself; give it away. You are called to go forth with a Fivefold anointing and give it away. When you receive the prophetic, give it away. When you receive the evangelistic, give it away. When you receive the pastoral anointing, give it away. Freely you have received; now freely give. Give what you receive away, and it will come back to you, good measure, pressed down, shaken together, and running over. There is multiplication when you give it away.

Where is the bottleneck in the body of Christ? Where is the multiplication? What are disciples doing with what they receive? Are they distributing it, or are they consuming it? The miracle is in the blessing, the breaking, and the giving. The miracle occurs when we give what we have been given. Jesus took it up and offered thanks. I know some people would say, "How could anything good come from this place, with these people?" This is what they said of Jesus: "Nazareth? Could anything good come from Nazareth?" But God says, "If you'll just give me five—not one or two, but five. Lift it, give thanks, break it, bless it, and give it. If you distribute it, I will multiply it."

Five is the number of grace. The grace of Christ is released when you begin to receive these twelve disciples. Twelve is the number of government, divine order, and apostolic government. When these twelve disciples began to receive the grace from the hands of Christ, they began to distribute it. Five thousand men, not counting the women and children, were fed. Do you want to see the masses fed? Do you want to see your region fed for the glory of God? Look past the natural. Open your spiritual eyes to see into the supernatural. See that God wants you to come under the Fivefold anointing. God wants you to be apostolic. You must

5: The Five Loaves

recognize you were not just born; you were sent to the earth for such a time as this.

God has sent you to bear the heart of the Father to the fatherless. He has sent you to share the love of the Father with those who don't have a father. God has sent you to arise in a prophetic anointing. God did not create you to depend on prophets; He wants you to hear the voice of the Lord for yourself. This is your season to begin to function and flow in the Fivefold anointing of the prophet. The prophetic anointing comes on you. This does not mean that you are a prophet, however you are stepping into maturity, so you hear the voice of the Lord with clarity. You can release the word of the Lord to someone on aisle 13 in Walmart or in Saks Fifth Avenue, at the gas pump, or at your job. You can release the word of the Lord that brings people into the Greater Glory!

Joshua Fowler

6

The Five Stones

Then he took his staff in his hand, and he chose for himself five smooth stones from the brook, and put them in a shepherd's bag, in a pouch which he had. And his sling was in his hand. And he drew near to the Philistine. 1 Samuel 17:40

We've read the story of David and Goliath many times, typically looking at it from the point of view of David, Goliath, Saul, or the children of Israel. I would like to present it to you from the stones' perspective. David chose five smooth stones. Keep in mind, five is the number of grace, it represents the Fivefold ministries: the apostle, the prophet, the evangelist, the pastor, and the teacher. Five smooth stones. Except the stones didn't start out that way.

Let's suppose a boulder on the side of a cliff, it falls off and crashes upon the ground, shattering into a million pieces of rock. Floods come and begin to carry the pieces of the boulder away. The water carries them into a great river, where they begin to crash against the banks and against one another. The rough edges on these stones are chipped away. Have you been feeling like that lately? The process of maturity isn't always fun. The river then carries the pieces of rock along until one day they are washed up on the riverbank. All they do is sit while the sun beats down on them. Imagine you are one of those pieces of rock. A builder comes looking for a stone; only he steps over you, picks up another stone, and says, "This one is more fitting for the house I'm about to build."

Then the waters begin to rise, the stones are carried away. At first, they are relieved to be moving in the water again. But then they begin crashing into one another and the riverbank just like before. More of their rough edges are being smoothed. These stones are crying, "Get me out of here! I want to be something. I want to be put in a house. I want to be used." As the years go by, the river carries the stones into a little stream, where they settle on the bottom. The clear water flows gently over them like a divine polisher. Are you immersed and settled in the washing of the water of God's Word?

One day, a shepherd boy comes to the stream. He is about to fight a giant. The king offered him his armor, although the boy didn't feel good about that. He decided to stick with his sling. He is now standing in the stream, looking for five smooth stones. He looks long and hard in the water for just the right stones. After all, this is a big giant, who also has several brothers. He picks up a stone saying, "This one looks like a pastor. This one will give that giant a push in the right direction." Then he puts it in his pouch. He picks up another stone. "Ah, this looks like a teacher. I think this one just might teach that giant a lesson!" He takes a few steps, picks up another. It looks good on one side, except when he turns it over, it is still rough. He throws it back in the water so it can go through the process of maturity. Just because you can preach doesn't mean you're ready to preach.

He picks up another stone saying, "Whoa! That looks like an evangelist. He's going to reach out and touch someone." Then he turns over stone after stone. Finally, he says, "I think this one will work. It looks like a prophet. This one will make the devil get the point!" He continues his search, feeling like something very important is missing.

"So, what am I missing? Ah, the apostle! Because the last shall be first and the first shall be last." The shepherd boy picks up one stone after another. "No, this one wants to lord over the people; it has a Saul, religious regime attitude. I'll throw it back in for a little while. It needs to go through some more floods. Oh, this one looks good, but it wants sons to give to him and he won't give to any sons." So, he throws that one back too. Finally, the shepherd boy picks up a stone, turns it over, examining it carefully. This stone has been at the bottom of the stream for years, being polished and smoothed over. The boy says, "This stone is like the apostle. It will hit the

6: The Five Stones

mark. It will bring God's order, His government, and His presence. Then all the other stones will be used mightily. ALL the giants will fall." The boy puts the last stone in his pouch, which represents the Fivefold centers God is raising up today.

For years, many gifts in the church have been isolated and overlooked. These ministers knew they were called. They knew they had gifts for the body of Christ. Then a spiritual father chose them. He put them in the pouch and set them down because to be sent, you must first sit. And you must sit until you're set. When you're set, the apostle can take you out of the bag and send you forth to fulfill your destiny. The Lord is building His church the way He wants to build it, as a family of fathers and sons, mothers and daughters, fathers and daughters, and mothers and sons.

> *Behold, children are a heritage from the LORD, the fruit of the womb is a reward. Like arrows in the hand of a warrior, so are the children of one's youth. Happy is the man who has his quiver full of them; They shall not be ashamed but shall speak with their enemies in the gate. Psalm 127:3-5*

The church is not going to establish what God wants us to establish just by confronting the enemy. We must also raise sons and daughters. God is establishing Fivefold centers with quivers full of arrows ready to hit the mark, to raise up this generation and the generations to come. If you will submit yourself to a father in the faith as a son and go through the process of sonship. If you will sit until you're set in the pouch. The day will come when the shepherd, your spiritual father, under God the Father's direction, will pull you out of the pouch and sling you at the giant!

David picked up that first stone called the apostle, and said, "This apostle, I'm going to send it forth." He then picked up the stone called the prophet, and said, "I'm going to send this prophet. He's going to point the way." Maybe he took the teacher and said, "I'm going to teach you a lesson." He might have taken the evangelist and said, "I'm going to reach out and touch someone." David took one of those Fivefold stones. Goliath was there taunting him for days. The Bible says David ran to meet Goliath, and he let that stone go. This is the moment when rock and roll began. That smooth stone hit Goliath on the head, and the giant rolled.

How will you take out the giants in your life? Receive this in your spirit. As you come under the Fivefold anointing and mature as a believer, you will know who you are! Jesus gave these gifts. Declare this aloud, "I receive the Fivefold."

You may ask, "How will we take Goliath out, in the city?" This will take place once we become Fivefold believers. The Fivefold is needed within our personal lives, families, and spheres of influence. This must be more than a Sunday church thing — it must become a lifestyle. The apostolic will bring order and unity to families. The prophetic will help believers see what is to come and speak what is to come. The pastoral and teaching anointing will help believers in obeying the Great Commission and discipling those around them. The evangelistic anointing will help believers, so they always bring a net with them to share the love of Jesus with their community and bring in the harvest. We must embrace the Fivefold culture. Every stronghold will come down as we walk in the fullness of Christ.

In the coming chapters we will dive deeper into each of the Fivefold Gifts so we can know better how to receive and flow with each of their distinct graces.

7

The Hand - The Five Fingers of God

Therefore, humble yourselves under the mighty hand of God, That He may exalt you in due time. 1 Peter 5:6

Over the years, I've heard of how other men and women of God have received revelation about the hand of God. Which has only confirmed what I received from the Lord as a teenager. I remember it like it was yesterday. I was just starting out as a youth pastor in an Assembly of God church in Panama City Beach, Florida. A few young leaders and myself felt led to go on a fast and shut in at our church. If you're not familiar with the old fashioned term, "shut in" well, it's where someone or a group of believers stay at a church or home and pray until they have prayed through! They are determined not to leave until they get what they've came for.

During this particular shut in, the Lord revealed many things to me, one of which was a vision of His Hand. I saw a hand moving across a field and what appeared to be a war-torn, barren land behind it. His Hand moved across the land with such violent velocity and fierce force that at first I was frightened. I assumed that His Hand was bringing destruction. Then the Lord said, "Look again, Son". As I looked again, The Vision unfolded and I saw the Hand was gathering the Harvest. Then in the distance I began to see this vast army of those who had been harvested taking their places and marching in rank and order behind The Hand. These people who were once lost in sin were now soldiers and harvesters in the army of the Lord. Many were worshipping with banners and shofars as they gathered the harvest with The Hand of God. The Lord went on to share with me that The Hand represented His Fivefold leaders and how they were equipping and leading His Church to gather the greatest Harvest of Souls of all times!

Take a moment and hold your hand out. Your hand represents the Fivefold. The apostle is the thumb which can touch all other four gifts. The prophet is the pointing finger which can point you to your future. The evangelist is the index finger which can reach the farthest. The ring finger is the pastor because he is married to the church. The teacher is the pinky finger which gets in those places to help ground us in truth. God wants you to know every time you look at your hand you need all 5 fingers. Have you ever tried to feed yourself with just two fingers? Some people must do it, but if not, aren't you thankful you have ten fingers and two hands? God gave you five so you can feed yourself. Have you ever tried to bathe yourself with two fingers? This is what most of the church has been doing. The pastor and the teacher or the pastor and the evangelist have been trying to feed and wash the church. Can you form a fist to punch with only two fingers? This is how we've been fighting. You need all five. Why? The apostle will bring the government to unite all five ministries together, so then you can form a fist to be victorious over the enemy!

In I Kings 18:44, there was a drought. The prophet Elijah told his servant to go back and forth seven times to look for rain. Returning from the seventh time, the servant said, "My Lord Elijah, I see a cloud like unto a man's hand." Do you want the rain of revival to be released on the earth? Elijah told his servant to get up and run because the rain was here! Are you a rain runner? It's raining! It's raining! The rain is here. The cloud likened to a man's hand is a prophetic picture of the Fivefold ministries of apostles, prophets, evangelists, pastors, and teachers. When we receive the Fivefold ministries together, the heavens will become heavy with rain. Elisha outran the chariot to Jezreel. Acceleration is here! You are in a sudden season! You are moving out of the land called stuck into a warp speed of a suddenly. As you receive the Fivefold anointing, you will rise and move forward!

> *Elijah was a man with a nature like ours. He prayed earnestly it would not rain; yet it did not rain on the land for three years and six months. James 5:17*

7: The Hand - The Five Fingers of God

The Lord is saying, "I want you to pray like Elijah." The effective fervent prayer of a righteous man avails much. I want you to pray until you see the rain come. I want you to pray until you see the fire fall. I want you to pray until you see the hand of God formed over your land! The Lord told me, "I'm going to raise up heralds that will begin to run for the rain and say, 'God's reign is here. God's reign is here.'" Reign is released in the rain. How is this going to happen? The Fivefold ministries are being brought together to flow together as the hand of God. We do not only need apostolic centers, prophetic centers, evangelistic centers, pastoral centers, and teaching centers, we need Fivefold centers. As we humble ourselves under the Hand of God (Fivefold), God will anoint us to gather the greatest harvest of all times!

> *I will teach you about the hand of God; what is with the Almighty I will not conceal. Job 27:11*

The hand brings revelation. It takes things that are hidden and concealed and opens them up to the body of Christ. It brings illumination and revelation so we can grow and reach maturity. Do you want to be fully mature in the Lord? I know I do! This will happen as we receive from the Hand of God.

Joshua Fowler

8

The Five G's

Now, let's look at these Fivefold ministry gifts. Let's explore how God is using them and why we need them. I'm going to give you what some call the Five G's of the Fivefold.

Teachers Ground us. You need to be grounded in the truth of God's Word, in the deep, rich soil of His truth. God uses teachers, that face of a man you can relate to, to help you be grounded in the truth of His Word. Do you want to be grounded in God's Word?

Next, Pastors Guard. God uses pastors to guard the flock, to keep them safe from wolves trying to come in and take them out, to protect them from consuming things they shouldn't be consuming — spiritually and otherwise. When the pastoral ministry is properly set up and carried out, it will protect your soul and your life. So, pastors guard.

Evangelists Gather. They teach us to go out and gather in the harvest. God wants you to help gather the harvest. He wants you to reach and extend. Every time you see your hand, especially your middle finger (which the enemy might try to use for other purposes), remember God wants you to extend yourself to gather the harvest. Now, you might say, "I'm not an evangelist." Well, God told Timothy to do the work of an evangelist. You don't have to be one to do the work of one.

If you become an apostolic, you'll want to bear the Father's heart to those who are fatherless on the earth. You'll desire to live a life of order. If you become prophetic, you won't just want a word — you'll want God to use you to deliver words to others. You'll be at the gas pump, and before you know it, God will be prophesying through you, giving you words of knowledge and wisdom because you've become a mature believer. Now, you give a word.

True prophets won't want you to depend on them. True prophets will help you mature so you can hear God for yourself, and you can prophesy. You can prophesy, so get that in your spirit. If you're truly mature, you'll become pastoral. You might say, "I'm a prophet, not a pastor." Well, that's the problem. You need to be balanced. You can't just point and prophesy all the time. You need to mature, love the sheep, and care for God's flock. Then, you'll prophesy out of that love, in balance.

If you're truly a mature believer, you'll step out and become a teacher. You'll realize what you've received isn't meant to be kept to yourself. You'll want to open your home, your coffee table, or take breaks at work to share the Word with others. You'll begin to give the Word to people in your sphere of influence so they can grow. We are apostolic, prophetic, evangelistic, pastoral, and we have a teaching anointing. We are raised up in maturity. Why? So, we can do the work of the ministry.

The Fivefold ministries are here to raise us up to do the work of the ministry. What is the work of the ministry? We are ambassadors of reconciliation. We are called by God — all of us — whether you have a pulpit ministry or not, to reconcile lost people back to God. We are all called to make disciples, not just the pastors, prophets, apostles, teachers, or evangelists. You've been ordained by God to raise up disciples.

Prophets Guide. They hear the Word of the Lord, see ahead, and help guide us. They also might warn us of the enemy's traps. Do you want guiding anointing in your life?

Finally, apostles Govern. There's a governmental grace and anointing on apostles. Look at your hand again. The thumb or apostle touches every other ministry gift but also brings them together, like a fist, so we can punch the enemy. Would you like to give the enemy a good punch and

8: The Five G's

knock him out? That's why the apostle is here—to bring us together to knock out the enemy.

When I was a kid, I took a couple of martial arts classes. I remember being taught when you punch, you need to make sure your thumb is on the outside. Don't put your thumb under the other fingers, or you'll break it. Similarly, some people want to put the apostle under the other ministry gifts, but that's not proper — it will break the hand. The apostle brings the hand together so you can punch the enemy and knock him out. Do you want to see the enemy knocked out of your life, out of your city, and out of this nation?

Have you ever tried to feed yourself with just two fingers? I'm not just talking about the thumb and the prophet. But for the most part, over the last 100 or even 1,000 years, from the Dark Ages onward, the church has tried to feed itself with less than the full Fivefold ministries. Most churches in America today only recognize a pastor, and occasionally an evangelist. They try to feed themselves with just two fingers.

Here's a challenge for you: Today at lunch, try picking up your fork with just two fingers. Ladies, try applying your makeup, and everyone, try brushing your teeth tonight with just two fingers. Men, try shaving with just two fingers. It's possible, except it's cumbersome. Ladies, imagine trying to shave your legs with just two fingers. Think about that—this is how much of the body of Christ has operated. They've tried to defend themselves with just two fingers. You might feel like Bruce Lee, but for the most part, it's not going to work. That's why God gave us all five.

You don't need just the pastor, the teacher, the evangelist, the prophet, or the apostle — you need all five. Dr. Bill Hamon said, "Any one fifth of us might get you drunk, but all five of us will get you strong, equipped, and mature." Do you desire to be strong, equipped, and mature? If so, you need all five ministry gifts. Let me insert this here: If you are truly a mature believer, you will have all these Fivefold anointings operating in your life. If you get under the hand of God, you'll become apostolic. You'll recognize you've been sent for such a time as this to reach those in your sphere of influence.

Most of the body of Christ is malnourished. Most of the body of Christ doesn't know much beyond sitting under a teacher and the occasional evangelist. This is why we're not reaping the harvest. This is why we're staying in our buildings, and many congregations are dwindling. They're getting older, with fewer generations and less harvest. Right now, many denominations in America are holding meetings about closing four churches in an area and combining them into one. Some large denominations have an average age groups in their 70s and the harvest is nowhere to be found. Why? Because many have continued to be fed without receiving from all Fivefold ministries. We need evangelists to come in — not just to preach us happy—but to equip us to go out and gather the harvest.

In this hour, you're not just going to sit in a seat and be a bobblehead believer. You're going to be raised up and equipped to do the work of an evangelist. You're not called to just attend church and receive an occasional prophecy from a prophet. You must hear God for yourself and to do prophetic evangelism outside the house of God. You can no longer just go to church, put money in the basket, and say, "You go to the nations." No, you're going to receive a sending anointing on your life. You're going to begin to go into the highways, the hedges, and yes, you will even join apostolic and prophetic teams and go to the nations. You cannot just sit in church, ever learning and never coming to the knowledge of the truth. You are required to become a mature believer so you can teach others what you learned yourself. This is what the true church, the Ecclesia is returning to in this hour.

In the early church, it was a privilege to be a part of the body. It was an honor. In fact, you couldn't just leave a church in those days and go across the street to find another one. There was one church, and if they met in different locations, they all knew one another. If you were excommunicated from one, you weren't a part of them. If they told you not to eat with someone, you wouldn't eat with them. Why? Because it was an honor to be part of the church, and you didn't just sit idly—you were a disciple, and you made disciples.

Yes, I believe the church needs to begin recognizing the privilege we have of being members of the body of Christ. We need to take it seriously. Have you ever been around a Muslim? Right in the middle of the day, they'll roll out their prayer mat and pray. Jehovah's Witnesses do it. Mormons do it. It's time for us, as the people of God, to take our faith seriously. We need to make disciples.

Some have said, "You can't call yourself an apostle or prophet. If you do, you're in pride." If calling yourself an apostle or prophet is pride, then why isn't it pride for an evangelist, pastor, or teacher to say who they are?"

Then, in 1992, the Lord came to me and said, "If you're ashamed of your calling, you're ashamed of Me. Walk boldly in your calling, and I will back it up with signs and wonders." So, in February 1992, as a 20-year-old, when someone asked me what I was called to be, I said, "I'm an apostle."

You should have seen how many places freaked out when I said that. But over time, God started sending prophets, apostles, and others to confirm my calling. Within two years, I started four churches. It was crazy. People started getting healed, delivered, and set free because I came into agreement with what God said about me. Do you want to come into agreement with what God says about you? Once you do, a fresh and greater anointing will be released in and through your life.

God wants to Dwell Among Us!

God wants you to understand the Fivefold ministries. Why do we need the Fivefold? In Psalm 68:18, it says: *"You have ascended on high, You have led captivity captive; You have received gifts among men, even from the rebellious, that the Lord God might dwell there."*

Why? Because God wants to dwell among His people. He wants to come and inhabit whole cities and territories. Why do we need these gifts that Christ received? As we see in Ephesians 4:8, Jesus led captivity captive and gave gifts to men. Why did He receive them, and why did He give them? Because God wants to dwell among His people.

You see this in Ephesians 4:8. Why do we need the Fivefold? To edify the saints! You don't have to be like the Catholic Church's version of a saint — you can be a believer and be a saint. The equipping of the saints, as stated in Ephesians 4:12.

We need the Fivefold ministries for longevity. The only way the kingdom of God will increase, grow, and continue is through the Fivefold. According to the same passage, the Fivefold brings the unity of the faith. How many believe we need some unity? I'm not talking about conformity — we don't all need to be the same. We need true unity. How many love it when there's unity and harmony in a band? That's a beautiful picture of unity. Somebody sings the melody, while others sing different parts; it makes a beautiful sound when we come together with our distinct voices.

The Fivefold also brings the knowledge of the Son of God. Do you desire to come into the knowledge of the Son of God? This is all in Ephesians chapter 4. Lastly, the Fivefold is necessary for maturity. God wants us to be mature.

Now, I didn't say "manure" — I said "mature," okay? I want you to understand the difference, because some people say they're mature yet sit in churches like bumps on logs. "I'm too mature to be passionate. When you get as mature as me, you won't have so much zeal. You won't be so excited. I used to be like you." There are people who say when new converts are excited, coming to church early and staying late. They say, "I used to be like you when I was first saved, only now I'm mature." No, you're not mature — that's manure. Because if you're truly mature, you'll keep your passion. You'll get more undignified than this. You won't sit

8: The Five G's

like a bump on a log—you'll say, "Come on, I'm here early, and you ain't seen nothing yet. I'm going to stay late. I'm going after God."

We will grow, and we will walk in maturity together. We will grow so we can see The Kingdom of God expanded in the earth.
Declare this with me: "We declare and decree we are Fivefold believers. We are apostolic, prophetic, evangelistic, pastoral, and teaching believers. We receive all five graces of God so we can be thoroughly supplied and equipped to do the work of the ministry. We decree it now in Jesus' name. Amen.

At 16 years old, the Lord downloaded the Fivefold ministry to me, telling me to study it. So, I spent two years studying the Fivefold. I call it my time at BBC aka "Bedroom Bible College". I stayed in my room, prayed, and devoured the Word, while most of my friends were out hanging around. I asked every leader I could find for wisdom: "Where are the apostles? Where are the prophets? What does this mean?" And the Holy Spirit taught me. God sent prophets like Mansfield Samples from Pontiac, Michigan—whom I called "Dad Samples" — and NH Dutton, the first prophet I ever received from.

Then one day, my mom and dad came home from a meeting at Christian International in Santa Rosa Beach, Florida and said, "We've met some people like you." They said, "They're meeting in these modular buildings off of Highway 98. You've got to go." So, one night, I went, and there were prophets. I'd never seen that many prophets in my life. They were gathering, equipping and training people. I was a little freaked out because I was still being set free from religiosity and tradition of men. I couldn't handle everything they were doing, to be honest. I watched it for a couple of hours and left. Later, the Lord brought that back around. Bishop Hamon became a dear friend. He invited me to eat, and we started spending time together. I ministered with him in America and Taiwan. Over the years, I have received a tremendous impartation from Dr. Hamon, Apostles Tom and Jane Hamon and many of the leaders from Christian International. Dr. Hamon is 90 years old and still preaching and prophesying.

I share this to say the Lord started showing me and opening Ezekiel to me. He showed me these faces: the face of a man, the face of an ox, the face of a lion, and the face of an eagle. He began to reveal what they represented, even though I didn't read this in a book. Dad Samples didn't teach it to me. Although the Lord used great men of God such as NH Dutton, Mansfield Samples and Bishop Hamon in a great way in my life, I did not receive this from a man. The Holy Spirit downloaded this into me as a young teenager crying out to Him.

The face of the lion represents the apostle. The apostle comes into a territory and brings order so the eagle — the prophet — has a place to land. For years, we've had churches with prophets, but then sometimes the ministry gifts there don't know how to receive the prophet, so there's no landing strip for them to come in and go out from. But God partners the apostle and the prophet. The lion is the king of the jungle, and the eagle is the king of the air. With Jesus Christ as the chief cornerstone, they form the foundation of the church. The ox represents the evangelist who brings in the harvest, and the man represents the pastor and teacher who bear the heart of God to mankind.

Why do we need lions and eagles? If you're thinking, "Lions and tigers and bears, oh my!" — This is about God wanting the church to be victorious and to conquer territory. He doesn't want us to be just gathering centers and holding tanks. He wants us to be commissioned and sent out. He puts apostles and prophets in the foundation of the church so the church will be a mobilized force taking the kingdom everywhere we go — to change our workplaces, education, government, and the world. This is what God calls the church to be. The church is a militant force. The word "church" is Ecclesia. He said, "Upon this rock, I will build my Ecclesia, my governing body." He didn't put us on earth to just peacefully coexist, gathering in a room singing "Kumbaya." He put us here to be trained, equipped, launched, and sent forth to take the land. That's why He places apostles and prophets in the foundation of the church. Over the coming

8: The Five G's

chapters we will spend a little time on The Five Porches and unpack the power of the Fivefold.

Joshua Fowler

9

The Five Porches

After this, there was a feast of the Jews, and Jesus went up to Jerusalem. Now in Jerusalem by the Sheep Gate a pool, which is called in Hebrew, Bethesda, having five porches. In these lay a great multitude of sick people, blind, lame, paralyzed, waiting for the moving of the water. For an angel went down at a certain time into the pool and stirred up the water. Then whoever stepped in first, after the stirring of the water, was made well of whatever disease he had. Now a certain man was there who had a disability for thirty-eight years. John 5:1-4

How many porches? Five porches. I believe Jesus positioned Himself prophetically and strategically for this miracle in the midst of the the five porches. It's not by chance He steps into Bethesda with five porches. He stepped into Bethesda, declaring, "My house has five porches!" My house has an Apostle's Porch. My house has a Prophet's Porch. My house has an Evangelist's Porch. My house has a Pastor's Porch. My house has a Teacher's Porch. You will find Christ in His fulness as you access all Five Porches!

In John 5, we see that this certain man had been suffering for thirty-eight long years. Many of us might have gone through something for a month, a year, five years, or maybe ten years. However, I don't know many people who have battled something for 38 years. Perhaps most of his life, he lay in that condition. Jesus said to the man lying by the pool, "Do you want to be made well?" This is what the Lord is saying to the church today, especially to the church in America. Do you want to be made well? The sick man replied, "I don't have anybody to put me in the water." I love how Jesus ignored him.

Jesus, in His loving mercy, said, "Rise, take up your bed, and walk." Jesus didn't even address the man's statement. Jesus was saying, "I am the well in the middle of the well. I am the living bread. I am the living water, and I'm here. You don't have to be put in the pool. I'm here. Come to Me and receive your healing."

Notice how Jesus intentionally chose to perform this miracle in the midst of the five porches. He was prophetically illustrating and demonstrating for the ages to come that all roads lead to me in the center. Just as we see in John 5 how these Five Porches all led to Jesus in the center of Pool of Bethesda, so will all true Fivefold ministries usher the people to Christ in the Center.

We also need to say, "I'm going to be rooted, grounded, and planted in the middle of the five porches. I will receive all five of the ministries."

John 5 is so profound, prophetic and practical. Jesus intentionally chose this specific place and time to reveal how the Ecclesia will come into His fullness and demonstrate His Kingdom as mature sons and daughters, When we access these Five Porches we will flow in the greater glory with signs, wonders and miracles following.

It's time for Bethesda Believers to arise! It's time for the paralyzed and immobile church to be fully equipped on all Five Porches. We need to stop looking for a man and receive God's Hand. We must frequent and dwell on all Five Porches.

I can see it, can you? Just imagine someone who was lost walking down the Evangelist's Porch and being led to Christ. Then once they are saved they are ushered from the Evangelist's Porch to the Pastor's Porch where they receive Sozo from the Shepherd's anointing. Then from there they are ushered to the Teacher's Porch where they are grounded and discipled in the Word of God. Then from there they are led to the Prophet's Porch where they are taught to hear the Lord for themselves and helped to discover their destiny. Then from there they are ready to go to the

9: The Five Porches

Apostle's Porch where they receive the Father's affirmation and are commissioned as sons and daughters into the Harvest fields. Then these Harvesters come in and out of the Five Porches bringing with them the harvest. As this takes place the church will grow both spiritually and numerically. More importantly, The Greater Glory that has been promised will be realized and released in and through the Ecclesia. Yes, His Glory shall cover the earth as the water covers the sea!

Joshua Fowler

10

The Apostle's Porch

Let's spend some time on the Apostle's Porch and discover the benefits of receiving apostolic ministry and impartation.

Strong's Dictionary Greek Definition of an Apostle:

g0651. ἀποστολή apostolē; from 649; commission, i.e. (specially) apostolate: — apostleship. AV (4) - apostleship 4; a sending away of the sending off of a fleet of consuls with an army, i.e. of an expedition

a sending away, i.e. a dismissal, release a thing sent, esp. of gifts in the NT, the office and dignity of the apostles of Christ, apostleship

g0652. ἀπόστολος apostolos; from 649; a delegate; specially, an ambassador of the Gospel; officially a commissioner of Christ ("apostle") (with miraculous powers) : — apostle, messenger, he that is sent.

Apostles are Commissioners!

So just from the Greek Definition of the word Apostle we can learn a lot. Jesus could have chosen any term to name his disciples, however he chose the word apostle. As you can see it's a military and ambassadorial term. God intentionally chose to send His Son as His Apostle to the earth in a time period where it would be understood. The Roman Empire was in full swing, so Christ chose the word apostle intentionally to show his disciples they were being sent forth by Him as a ambassadors to represent Him and His Kingdom. Apostles are commissioners. They have been commissioned to commission and sent to send forth leaders and believers into their divine assignments and callings. When you get around them you will be stirred up and sent forth to fulfill your destiny.

And my speech and my preaching were not with persuasive words of human wisdom. But in demonstration of the Spirit and of power, that your faith should not be in the wisdom of men but in the power of God. 1 Corinthians 2:4-5

Then fear came upon every soul, and many wonders and signs were done through the apostles. Acts 2:43

And with great power, the apostles gave witness to the resurrection of the Lord Jesus, and great grace was upon them all. Acts 4:33

Mega Favor accompanies Apostles!

The apostles flowed with great power. They gave witness to His resurrection, and then great grace came upon the church. Great grace is released through apostolic ministry. In the Greek, this "great grace" means "mega favor." Could you use some mega favor? Great Grace or Mega Favor accompanies the ministry gift of apostles.

Look at Acts 5:1-16, Romans 15:18-19, and 1 Thessalonians 1:10. All of these passages reiterate the signs, wonders, and miracles that happen through the apostolic ministry. What do apostles do? They edify; they build up the church (Ephesians 4:12). They bring revelation to the body of Christ (Ephesians 3). What do apostles bring to your life? Why do you need an apostle? Why should you sit under the ministry of an apostle or bring apostles to your church? I'll tell you why. Here's what they unpack:

Apostles and Prophets unlock Mysteries!

How that by revelation He made known to me the mystery, as I have briefly written already, by which, when you read, you may understand my knowledge in the mystery of Christ. Which in other ages was not made known to the sons of men, as it has now been revealed by the Spirit to His holy apostles and prophets. Ephesians 3:3-5

Having been built on the foundation of the apostles and prophets, Jesus Christ, the chief cornerstone, in whom the whole building,

10: The Apostle's Porch

fitted together, grows into a holy temple in the Lord. In whom you also are being built together for a dwelling place of God in the Spirit. Ephesians 2:20-22

According to the grace of God, which was given to me, as a wise master builder I have laid the foundation, and others build on it. But let each one take heed of how he builds on it. For no other foundation can anyone lay than that which is laid, which is Jesus Christ. 1 Corinthians 3:10-11

God uses apostles and prophets to help us understand our inheritance and to release mysteries. They bring forth revelation. God uses apostles as part of the foundation.

1. **Apostles are Master Builders:** According to 1 Corinthians 3:9-10, apostles are like architects or general contractors. They see the whole plan, while others might only see part of it.

2. **Apostles Set Doctrinal Order:** You can see this in Acts 15:2, 4, 6, 22, 23, and again in Acts 16:4. Apostles set doctrinal order. This doesn't happen because a college of bishops comes together to figure something out intellectually. This happens because the ministry gift of the apostle sets that order. What do they bring? Apostolic doctrine. Acts 2:42 says, "And they continued steadfastly in the apostles' doctrine and fellowship, in the breaking of bread, and in prayers." Notice, it starts with the apostles' doctrine.

3. **Apostles Correct Error:** Much of the epistles were written by the apostles to correct error. They dealt with issues in the church.

4. **Apostles Equip:** Apostles equip the saints to do the work of ministry. Ephesians 4:11-16

Fathering and Sonship

This dimension of the apostolic is necessary for the growth of the Kingdom. Yes, we are sheep; we need shepherds, yet we are also sons and daughters, and we need fathers and mothers. We need the patriarchs and matriarchs to arise in our churches to raise up sons and daughters in the Kingdom.

> *For I think God has displayed us, the apostles, last, as men condemned to death; for we have been made a spectacle to the world, both to angels and to men. We are fools for Christ's sake, but you are wise in Christ; we are weak, but you are strong; you are distinguished, but we are dishonored. To the present hour we both hunger and thirst, and we are poorly clothed, and beaten, and homeless. And we labor, working with our own hands. Being reviled, we bless; being persecuted, we endure; being defamed, we entreat. We have been made as the filth of the world, the offscouring of all things until now. 1 Corinthians 4:9-15*

Now, who wants to sign up to be an apostle? The enemy wants to promote the apostle as a title, only it's not about a title. You don't need a title; you need a towel to serve the sons and daughters. The Apostle Paul said, "I bear the marks." In my 37 years of preaching, I have marks from stepping out and blazing trails to help establish this on the earth. Being an apostle is not about getting a title to put on your website or social media. If you're an apostle, you're going to lay your life down as a foundation for others to build on. You might be defamed; you might be the offscouring.

> *I do not write these things to shame you, but as my beloved children, I warn you. For though you might have ten thousand instructors in Christ, yet you do not have many fathers; for in Christ Jesus, I have begotten you through the gospel. Therefore, I urge you, imitate me. For this reason, I have sent Timothy to you, who is my beloved and faithful son in the Lord, who will remind you of my ways in Christ, as I teach everywhere in every church. I Corinthians 4:14-21*

This is a father walking tall with a big stick, knocking the devil out and raising up sons and daughters so they can fulfill their destiny. We need this fathering dimension.

10: The Apostle's Porch

Apostles Bring Impartation

Acts 8:14-19 shows apostles reveal who they are. When you're around apostles, you'll receive apostolic grace in your life (Romans 1:11; 1 Timothy 4:14; 2 Timothy 1:6). Apostle's stir up the gift of God in you. They function and raise up all the Fivefold ministries.

1. **Apostles Function as Evangelists:** The apostles didn't just function as apostles. They could also touch that evangelistic gift and raise up evangelists. They say, "This is how you do it. Follow me; this is how you win souls." They train and equip. **Acts 2:37-41; Acts 4:4, 11:21, 16:5, and 14:31-34**—All these passages show apostles in the book of Acts functioning and moving forward as evangelists.

2. **Apostles Function as Pastors and Teachers:** You see this in Acts 1:1, 4:18, 13:1, and 28-30. These are just a few examples, although there are many more. Apostles help pastor and shepherd the flock of God. Be careful how you take care of the flock of God for whom Jesus shed His blood. These were the apostles' words—an admonition to shepherd the flock. This is how an apostle, like James, can be part of a church, helping shepherd the flock while still being an apostle.

3. **Apostles Function as Prophets:** You see Peter doing this in Matthew 16 :13-19, Acts 5 :1-5, Acts 10 :9-20, 5-12, and Acts 12 :7-11. In all these passages, Peter flows in a prophetic dimension. How many believe apostles should flow prophetically? They touch that pointing finger—the prophet's finger—and help raise up the prophetic. Why do they need to function in it? So, they can help commission it. If apostles can't see the prophetic, they would only raise up others like themselves, but we need all five of the Fivefold ministries. You also see Paul functioning prophetically in Acts 9:1-7, 13:1-4, 15:30-32, 16:6-10, 18:9, 22:17-20, and 23:11, Acts 27:9-12, 21; and 2 Corinthians 12:1-4 are other examples of the Apostle Paul flowing prophetically, having visions, seeing angels, and

encountering the third heaven. These things are not just for prophets. There are people teaching today that there should be a separation of apostles and prophets, creating two different camps. They aren't reading the Bible. All these gifts were given by God to serve together in the church.

No Separation

There shouldn't be an apostolic camp, a prophetic camp, a pastoral camp, a teaching camp, or an evangelistic camp. There should be Fivefold Camp or Center which is the Church of the Lord Jesus Christ, where all five porches function together. There should be no separation of apostles and prophets. Apostles are prophetic. Some have tried to make apostles mere administrators.

Pomp vs. Power

Some organizations in America ordain or consecrate apostles as they do bishops. They anoint their thumbs and toes, put a big fish-head hat on their head like in the Catholic Church, dress them in robes, hand them a staff, and give them a big cross to wear. They walk them around the room, sit them in a big chair, and call them an apostle. That is not how you commission an apostle. You will not find this taking place anywhere in the New Testament. These are man-made traditions that are more full of pomp than power.

It's not about a title, it's about a towel!

Jesus never gave the apostles a big cross and a hat. He gave them a basin and a towel and washed their feet. He commissioned them to go and be apostles. It was not about the title, the hat, or the robes; it was about the heart of a servant. The Apostle Paul said, "Don't say, 'I am of Paul, and 'I am of Apollos.'" No, we are one. Prophets, you need to recognize true apostles won't lessen, squash, control, manipulate, or push you down. A true apostle will lay his life down to be a launching pad for you. Apostles, you should receive prophets because they release the Word of the Lord so you can decree it and see it come to pass.

Apostles Commission and Ordain

The apostles commission and ordain others. Jesus commissioned them in Luke 6. You see this again in Mark 3:13-19, where He commissioned the twelve. Throughout Acts, the apostles ordained deacons, elders, and bishops, also all the Fivefold ministry gifts. You can see this in Acts 6, Acts 14, Titus 1:5, 1 Timothy 3:1-16, 2 Timothy 4:22, and Titus 1:7. Paul had the grace of God to commission. Apostles have been commissioned by God with an anointing to commission you and I to gather the harvest and flow in the Greater Glory.

We need apostles, not denominational boards and organizations that aren't apostolic. We need true apostles who have the anointing of God to bring forth the other Fivefold ministries so we can lay hands on people and send them forth to fulfill their calling.

God's Chiropractors — Apostles and Apostolic Alignment

Several years ago, I experienced the worst pain I ever experienced in my life. It felt like a knife was piercing my lower back going down through my hip, and into my thigh. I thought about going to a chiropractor; however, I'd never been to one; many family members and friends told me horror stories about them. After weeks of fear robbing me of sleep and discomfort keeping me from day-to-day activities, the pain outweighed my fear of going to a chiropractor. I broke down and went to see one I knew was a Christian. I told him he'd better not mess me up because I knew his pastor! After reviewing my X-rays, he told me my back was out of alignment and asked me to lie down on his table. To correct what was causing the pain, he said he had to bring my whole body into alignment. SNAP, CRACKLE, POP, and POP, POP, POP. I felt like I was the victim in a kung-fu film! He proceeded to contort my body in all different directions, pulling, pushing, and then again - you guessed it - SNAP, CRACKLE, POP, and POP, POP, POP! When he said, "Okay, you can get up now," I was too scared to move. As I began to get up, I winced, "It still hurts. When will it get better?" He said, "This is going to take a while. I need to see you three times a week for at least the next three weeks."

Well, I had gone in with this misconception of one visit, a few pops, and no more pain. WRONG! And my attitude didn't get better. I was not exactly the model patient! After each visit I would go home whining about how it hurt worse. My wife would shake her head in dismay and say, "It will take a while baby, and you'll be back to normal." There were those who were right there, saying, "You see! I told you not to go to a chiropractor!" I was beginning to wonder if the pain would ever go away. But the day finally came when it began to subside; I began to see the light at the end of the tunnel. After a few months my spine came into alignment and the pain went away. That was over three years ago; I am still pain free today. I try to see my chiropractor regularly because it's better to stay in alignment than to get out! I think it's interesting that chiropractors have only begun to be accepted by the medical establishment and insurance companies. What they do is align the entire body so all the systems of the body can operate properly with one another. Does this sound familiar? Has the body of Christ been out of alignment? Have we been in pain, in desperate need of healing? Are we split into factions, each looking out only for its own interests?

In the last few years, God has been restoring the ministry of the apostle to properly align us and heal us. Can you see that? Apostolic alignment causes the same result in the body of Christ that natural alignment causes in the natural body: every joint supplies and the healing begins! This produces communication, cooperation, and understanding; and believers come into their divine destiny and fulfill the call of God.

Many believers fight the apostolic movement because, like I was with chiropractors, they are afraid of something new; some friends and family members are telling them to beware. Apostles come in and rock the boat, shake up old ways of thinking, and lambaste traditions of men. They have great vision; they run hard and long. All this gives much ammunition to those who don't believe God is restoring the apostles and prophets to the Church today! Reading and studying the biblical truths in this book will help you decide where you stand. The prophet Ezekiel saw a vision of dry bones coming together in Ezekiel 37. I believe as we continue to receive apostolic adjustments from God's apostles, we will see the dry bones of the Church come together in apostolic alignment. The Bible tells us what will happen.

> *From whom the whole body, joined and knit together by what every joint supplies, according to the effective working by which every part does its share, causes growth of the body for the edifying of itself in love. Ephesians 4:16*

This is the chiropractic scripture verse of the Bible! The whole body is joined together properly, every joint supplies, every part works effectively, and every believer walks in the love of God. I don't know about you; I'm ready for the body of Christ to come into that alignment!

The Ministry of the Apostle

In 1987 God called me to be an apostle. For years, I found myself shrinking back in false humility. Did you know false humility is just as much pride as pride is? I found myself shrinking back, thinking, when asked what I was called to be I would respond in false humility with answers such as, "I'm a church planter or I'm one called to pioneer." Then, the Lord came to me in February of 1992, when I was in my twenties. He said, "If you're ashamed of your calling, you're ashamed of me." He said, "If you walk boldly in your calling, I will back it up with signs, wonders, and miracles." So, in 1992, as a 20-year-old kid, when people asked me what I was called to be, I said, "I'm an apostle." They said, "Do you mean you're going to be?" I said, "No, I am one." They would ask, "How do you know you are one?" I would say, "Because the Lord walked into my room; I saw him with my eyes. He called me to be an apostle to the nations."

Some would look at me like well maybe one day when you grow up, when you become bald or when you have gray hair. Maybe one day you'll arrive and call yourself an apostle. Well, take that up with Abram when God told Abraham to call himself Abraham before he had any children. God said, "You're Abraham. Tell everybody you're Abraham." There were no kids around him, yet he was still Abraham. He was prophesying and speaking forth his destiny. Within a matter of months, I planted two churches by accident. Before we knew it, another church was born, and another church was born. I showed up to a town by invitation without a plan. One church was started in an old bank building in Clarksville, TN. Another church started in a hotel ballroom in Huntsville, AL. Two more churches in a church building and a hotel ballroom in Missouri. Two more churches in a house and another in a garage in Mexico. Two more churches in Russia in meeting halls and two more in South Africa. The list goes on and on! Miracles would break out! We had a young deaf boy at 7 years old that had never spoken or heard in his life. We prayed for him in the name of Jesus. The Lord opened his ears, and he said, "Mama!" for the first time!

I remember going to different conferences in different places dressed in a T-shirt and jeans. They would call me up to prophesy, and they would try to declare I was something other than who God called me to be. They would ask, "Does that make sense to you?" I would reply, "No. It really doesn't make any sense." They would ask, "Well, what are you?" I said, "I'm an apostle." "You mean you're going to be?" I said, "No, I am." They said, "Well, how old are you? What do you do for a living?" I would reply, "I'm 25 years old. I'm preaching the gospel. I've planted churches in different parts of the world."

I remember returning to preach at that place a month later as a conference speaker. After the meeting was over, the guy that thought I could not be an apostle came up to me and grabbed my bags. He said, "Oh, man of God. Oh, man of God. I see the anointing on you." Rather than looking with the eyes of the spirit earlier when I had a T-Shirt and jeans on, now after seeing me minister he could see. Wearing jeans and a T-shirt or a suit are not signs of the anointing. We must increase with spiritual vision to see beyond the natural outer appearance.

I finished signing books, then I walked out to the car. As the guy was carrying my bags, he said, "Oh, I'm just so honored to be with you." I looked at him and said, "Do you know what your problem is? You judge with the outward appearance; you don't look in the spirit. If you want to be accurate in the prophetic, you must stop looking with your eyes and look in the spirit." He's still my friend today because I rebuked him in love.

Not Many Fathers

> *For though you might have ten thousand instructors in Christ, yet you do not have many fathers; For in Christ Jesus, I have begotten you through the gospel. 1 Corinthians 4:15*

Paul is saying he has begotten the Corinthians through the gospel. His relationship with them is not just as a great teacher or orator who comes in occasionally to release knowledge. He is their father in the faith. He watches over them to see they are fed good food from the Word of God and corrects them when they get off into error. He holds them accountable to live by the Word and follow the Spirit. He loves them and prays for them like a natural father. But he is more than this! An apostle is a father in the faith who carries God's vision and has territorial authority. Apostles direct and vision to release divine destinies. One of the characteristics of apostolic alignment is being accountable to and coming into submission to a father in the faith. Our vision and divine destiny are supernaturally linked with their vision and divine destiny. The Bible talks a lot about fathers and sons, so we need to get something straight right now. Although the words used are "father and son," you can exchange those words for "mother and daughter" or "father and daughter" or "mother and son."

> *For as many of you as were baptized into Christ have put on Christ. There is neither Jew nor Greek, There is neither slave nor free, there is neither male nor female; for you are all one in Christ Jesus. Galatians 3:27-28*

In this hour of the Church, we are already seeing men and women apostles, just like they existed in the early church. We are seeing every kind of gender relationship in God's apostolic order and government because God is no respecter of persons. So, if you've had a problem with no "male nor female," I'm challenging you to embrace God's Word. Get past the old prejudice, so you can move into apostolic anointing and authority and fulfill your divine destiny. Within every believer lies a divine vision and destiny. Apostles gather those divine visions and destinies together to accomplish God's greater plan. That's what Paul meant when he said we have many teachers, pastors, counselors, mentors, and prayer partners. But we have few fathers and mothers who are appointed by God to raise up sons and daughters and send them forth to take territories and nations for the Kingdom of God.

Set by God and Given by Christ

And God has appointed these in the church: first apostles, second prophets, third teachers, after that miracle, then gifts of healings, helps, administrations, varieties of tongues. 1 Corinthians 12:28

And He (Christ) Himself gave some to be apostles, some prophets, some evangelists, and some pastors And teachers, for the equipping of the saints for the work of ministry, for the edifying of the body of Christ. Ephesians 4:11-12 (insert added)

Longevity

Know in your spirit apostles are not a dispensational gift that ended with the early church. Some teach that there are no longer apostles. They say there were only 12 apostles. What about Matthias, the 13th apostle, and Paul, the 14th? What about Barnabas, the 15th, or Junia, a female apostle mentioned in Romans 16:7? What about Timothy, who was also called an apostle? The Greek word used for Timothy was "messenger." If you keep going, there are at least 28 different apostles in the New Testament alone.

Apostles never ceased.

If someone argues cessationism, refer them to 1 Corinthians 13:8-10 and James 1:25. When they say there were only twelve, just ask them about the others. It's a perpetual gift. Jesus "gave" (1 Corinthians 12:28). Ephesians was written 20 years later, yet it still says He gave apostles to the church. Why would He say they were given if they had ceased?

10: The Apostle's Porch

1. **God Set Apostles:** 1 Corinthians 12:28
2. **Christ Gave Apostles:** Ephesians 4:11

If someone argues with you about this, just ask them, "Where in the Bible does it state God repealed the order? Where does it say that we don't need apostles and prophets anymore?"

True vs. False Apostles

You can see this distinction in 2 Corinthians 11:3-15.

These passages tell us God set apostles in the Church. Christ gave apostles to the Church, and not a place recorded in Scripture where our Father and Savior took them out or snatched them back from us. Some people believe apostles are not for today. They base their belief on a couple of scriptures. However, I have never found a biblical argument that soundly proved apostles (and prophets) have "passed away." If you study this subject in depth, I believe you will come to the same conclusion. In 1 Corinthians 12:28, apostles are set "first." The Greek word for "first" is *proton,* which means "first (in time, place, order, or importance): -before, at the beginning, chiefly (at, at the) first (of all). This definition does not mean apostles are better than the other ministry gifts. However, it does reveal the specific anointing apostles carry to blaze trails for others to come in and build the house of God. It paints the picture of arriving first, like the tip of an arrow. Apostles possess a *"proton* anointing" blasting the way to victory in cities, regions, and nations. And wherever you find this *proton* anointing, the body of Christ will experience tremendous breakthroughs, such as they did at Ephesus when Paul came on the scene with the *proton* anointing.

Catalyst for the Supernatural

And God has appointed these in the church: first apostles, second prophets, third teachers, after that miracle, then gifts of healings, helps, administrations, varieties of tongues. 1 Corinthians 12:28

In this verse something significant takes place after God sets "first apostles, secondarily prophets, thirdly teachers." What comes next? "After those miracles, then gifts of healings." Have you ever wondered why many times we don't witness miracles when we pray? I hear people all over the world saying, "I want to see a move of God." I reply to them, "If you want a move of God, you must move with God!"

Believers desire God's power, although many are unwilling to operate according to His principles. You see, if we want the power of the book of Acts, we must have the passion and presence of the book of Acts. To have the presence, we must learn to operate according to the principles of Acts. God's principles produce His presence, and His presence produces His power!

After the governmental structure of the Church is in place, we will witness the greatest outpouring of miracles, healings, and deliverance in history. I am convinced we will never experience the miraculous as believers did in the New Testament until we see the restoration of proper Church government. That word "until" is a powerful word.

> *Whom heaven must receive until the times of restoration of all things, which God has spoken by the mouth of all His holy prophets since the world began. Acts 3:21*

There must be a restoration of ALL things for us to see the Lord. Selah! Just think about it - God's been about the business of restoration for a long time! Many things were lost to or stolen from the Church over the years because religious traditions crept in taking the place of the truth. What I call "Operation Restoration" began with Martin Luther almost five hundred years ago and continues to this day. When he nailed his "Ninety-Five Theses" on the church door, the deception that for centuries clouded the Church's perception of Christianity began to dissipate.

In just this past century we have witnessed the restoration of tongues, healing, and so much more of the supernatural. Over the last three decades God has been restoring the governmental structure of the Church. In the seventies we began to see the restoration of the ministry of the teacher.

10: The Apostle's Porch

Ministers such as Kenneth Hagin, Kenneth and Gloria Copeland, Norvel Hayes, Jerry Savelle, and many others have been raised up to ground the body of Christ in the truth of God's Word.

In the eighties we began to see the restoration of the ministry of the prophet. Prophets such as Dr. Bill Hamon, Rick Joyner, Chuck Pierce, Cindy Jacobs, Kim Clement, and many others have come on the scene to bring clarity to the Church's destiny. These prophets have also taught us how to hear the voice of God for ourselves and prophesy to one another properly. In the nineties we began to see the restoration of the ministry of the apostle. Fellow apostles such C. Peter Wagner, Che Ahn, John Eckhardt, John Kelly and many others have brought understanding about the apostolic reformation that is taking place in the earth today. When we look over the past decades, we can see a rapid increase in the momentum of Operation Restoration that started with Martin Luther.

In 1 Corinthians 4:9, the apostle Paul says, "For I think God hath set forth us the apostles last." Then, in 1 Corinthians 12:28, he says, "God hath set ... first apostles." So, which is it? Both! They were set first and are being restored last. In Luke 13:30 Jesus said the first would be last and the last would be first. We are witnessing this phenomenon in the restoration of the Fivefold ministry gifts to the Church. When Jesus ascended to heaven after His resurrection, He left the Church in the hands of His apostles. I know what comes to mind - those old Last Supper paintings depicting twelve grumpy, old men breaking bread with the Lord. However, the artists got it wrong. Historians tell us the apostles were in their twenties and thirties at the time of the Last Supper. Most scholars believe John the Beloved was only in his late teens! (That will pop the religious bubbles of the works crew.) Apostles are not chosen by their age; they are simply chosen and anointed by God to be apostles. You're going to experience a tremendous anointing and manifestation of the supernatural around apostles. Moreover, apostolic alignment operates by grace, not works. Apostolic ministry is not about how many years you've been in ministry, how many people are following you, or how many churches you oversee. Nor does having a title of bishop make you an apostle. An apostle is a gift of grace that is commissioned to the body of Christ to commission God's people into their places of service.

> *O Jerusalem, Jerusalem, the one that kills the prophets and stones those who are sent to her! How often wanted to gather your children together, as a hen gathers her brood under her wings, but you We're not willing! See, your house is left to you desolate and assuredly, I say to you, you shall not See Me until the time comes when you say, Blessed is He who comes in the name of the Lord! Luke 13:34-35*

In essence Jesus was saying, "You mistreated my prophets and those I sent, so you will not see Me again until (there's that word again) you receive the sent ones." I believe that this not only refers to the return of Christ, it also directly relates to receiving Christ, the Anointed One, and those He has sent to represent Him in the earth. Once we recognize and receive those God is sending, we will experience a powerful anointing and the greatest move of God of all times!

The Foundation of the Church

> *Having been built on the foundation of the apostles and prophets, Jesus Christ Himself being the chief cornerstone. Ephesians 2:20*

Apostles and prophets are the foundation of the Church. Our adversary knows if he can take away our foundation, then he can destroy the whole house. Nevertheless, the house of God stands sure! All over the world leaders and believers are discarding hand-me-down religion and are embracing God's apostles. Churches are growing stronger because of returning to the biblical foundation of the apostles and prophets. We can see why and how apostles and prophets are the foundation for the Church in Ephesians 3:1-5. The apostle Paul explains God reveals "the mystery" to the apostles and prophets.

> *For this reason, I, Paul, the prisoner of Christ Jesus for you Gentiles— if indeed you have heard of the dispensation of the grace of God, which was given to me for you, how that by revelation He made known to me the mystery (as I have briefly written already, by*

10: The Apostle's Porch

which, when you read, you may understand my knowledge in the mystery of Christ), which in other ages was not made known to the sons of men, as it has now been revealed by the Spirit to His holy apostles and prophets. Ephesians 3:1-5

Bible scholars who believe apostles and prophets are passed away argue Ephesians 3:1-5 is speaking only of the redemptive work of Jesus; nothing else. But if you will do a word study on mystery, you will see that this term encompasses all the revelation and experience regarding Jesus Christ and His Church. It will take eternity to explore the depth and breadth of the mystery, which God is continuously revealing through the apostles and prophets in the Church today. Fresh revelation brings order and God's government to the body of Christ. A powerful word from the Lord gives the Church strategies and wisdom for the present. For too long we have attempted to accomplish things without this first, pioneering, breakthrough anointing of the apostle.

Many believers, calling themselves missionaries, have gone into new territories to establish a work of God without the proton anointing of an apostle. God has extended grace to us in our ignorance, and these attempts produced fruit. But consider how much more could have been accomplished with the assistance of God's apostles. If I need to dig a hole, why would I dig it myself with a little shovel and turn away the help of another who operated a backhoe? This is exactly what many leaders do when they refuse the assistance of apostles and prophets. There are many reasons for this: fear, jealousy, and control issues head the list. But they are all dispelled when we understand God has called us to work together. God gives apostles and prophets insight and revelation for building His house.

Apostles are the spiritual architects and visionaries of the Church. They are the master builders whom the Chief Cornerstone directs in the construction of His Temple - we are the temple of God. God has graced apostles as general contractors to work with a panoramic view (from prophets) with other the other contractors (evangelists, pastors, and teachers) to build the church according to His design.

> *For we are God's fellow workers; you are God's field, you are God's building. According to the grace of God, which was given to me, as a wise master builder I have laid the foundation, and another builds on it. But let each one take heed of how he builds on it. For no other foundation can anyone lay than that which is laid, which is Jesus Christ. 1 Corinthians 3:9-11*

Apostles and prophets lay the foundation and comprise the foundation for the Church (see Ephesians 2:20). Jesus, the Chief Cornerstone and Great Apostle upon whom the foundation is laid, told us exactly of what that foundation would consist of.

> *He said to them, "But who do you say that I am?" Simon Peter answered and said, "You are the Christ, the Son of the living God." Jesus answered and said to him, "Blessed are you, Simon Bar-Jonah, for flesh and blood has not revealed this to you, but My Father who is in heaven. And I also say to you that you are Peter, and on this rock I will build My church, and the gates of Hades Shall not prevail against it. Matthew 16:15-18*

In the Greek language, Peter's name means the fragment of a large rock. But the word Jesus uses for "rock" in verse 18 means "a massive boulder."2 That massive boulder is the revelation of who Jesus Christ is, and it is that revelation that constitutes the foundation of the Church. It is the revelation of the Lord Jesus Christ that will crush the enemy and every vile, deception, trap, and all-out attack of the powers of darkness. It is true that no vision rests on just one person's shoulders, yet all visions rest on the shoulders of the Lord Jesus Christ!

Generals of War

Apostles are generals in the army of the Lord. They get the battle plan from the Captain of the Host, hear what the prophets are saying, and carry out the plan. They pull their troops together, release gifts into the body, and set them in God's rank and file. We must arise as a Fivefold army,

10: The Apostle's Porch

operating in the proton anointing. When we do nothing will stop us from experiencing breakthrough in cities and nations for Jesus Christ!

Over the last 37 years, the Lord has revealed a lot to me about apostles and the apostolic calling on my life. So much so that I think I will dedicate an entire book to this subject. In fact, much of what I shared in this book was in my first book, Access Granted that I wrote in the 90's and published in 2002. Including these 24 Apostolic Traits that I will leave you with to continue your study.

Twenty-four Apostolic Traits

1. Divine Order - Joel 2; Psalm 133

2. Governments - 1 Corinthians 12:28; Isaiah 9:6-7

3. Fathering & Sonship - 1 Corinthians 4:9-21; 9:1-2; Galatians 4:19; 1 Timothy 1:2,18

4. Sent Sense - Romans 10:13-15; Acts 13:2-4; Luke 4:18-19

5. Pioneering Anointing - 1 Corinthians 12:28

6. Breakthrough Anointing - Micah 2:13; Isaiah 45:1-4; 2 Samuel 5:20

7. Operate in and Activate Others in Great Grace Acts 4:33

8. Equip and Establish - Ephesians 4:11-16; Acts 16:4-5

9. Defend the Faith - Philippians 1:17; Jude 3; 1 Peter 3:15

10. Team Ministry - Acts 21:8; Matthew 10:5-8; Luke 10:1-2

11. Usher in New Sounds from Heaven in Praise and Worship - Acts 16:25

12. Warfare Prayer Anointing - 2 Corinthians 10:3-6; Ephesians 6:10-18

13. Commissioning Anointing - Ephesians 4:11; Acts 13:2-4

14. Troublemakers - Acts 16:19-20, 17:6; John 8:58-59; Luke 23:5

15. Building Anointing - 1 Corinthians 3:10-11; Isaiah 58:12 and 61:1-7

16. Joshua Anointing to Cross Over into the Promised Land - Joshua 1 and 3

17. Finishing Anointing - Hebrews 12:1-5; 2 Timothy 4:7-8

18. Kingdom Authority and Power - 1 Corinthians 2:45, 4:20

19. Miracles, Signs, and Wonders - 2 Corinthians 12:12

20. Strategist - 2 Corinthians 10:3-6

21. Multicultural and Multinational- Micah 4:11-12; Isaiah 2:1-4; Acts 1:8, 17:26

22. Transgenerational - 1 Corinthians 4:15-17; Genesis 50:24; Proverbs 13:22

23. Great Patience - 2 Corinthians 12:12

24. Raise Up a Davidic Company to Minister unto the Lord - Acts 13:2-4, 21-22; 15:16-17; Isaiah 56:7

Declaration: "We declare, and we decree we receive the ministry gift of the Apostle. We receive the apostolic anointing that You have for our lives to build Your kingdom and establish Your church. We declare and decree that we will go to the Apostle's Porch and be commissioned as sons and daughters with the Father's heart! We will not be hearers only; we will be doers of Your word, In Jesus name, Amen."

11

The Prophet's Porch

Let's spend some time on the Prophet's Porch and discover the benefits of receiving prophetic ministry and impartation.

Over the years, I've helped train thousands of people in the prophetic. I've had the honor of helping to raise up many prophets and apostles. This is one of the primary things the Holy Spirit has revealed to me to equip others in. Primarily because there's been such a need for apostles and prophets to be restored. I've learned what to do and what not to do. One of the first things the Lord did with me was to put me in a house with two roommates who were prophets. I had to learn how to deal with their attitudes and emotions. They would feel things and see things, and they would get down and depressed because of what they saw in the spirit. I had to tell them, "Come on, get up out of that funk. You're just the messenger. You are the delivery person. Don't hold on to that. Don't be down because of what you saw or heard. Give it to Jesus."

Soul Control is essential!

Early on I got to witness and experience this first hand with two young minister friends who were my roommates. Both of them were emerging prophets and they were emotional roller coasters. They felt, sensed, and heard everything around them. One day, they were on a high, feeling great; the next day, they were so grieved they couldn't cope. Although this is part of growing in the prophetic, you still must remember you are a spirit who possesses a soul that lives in a body. Your soul must come under your spirit. You must have soul control. As a prophet, this is so important. You must learn to see it, hear it, know it, take it to the Lord, and leave it there. Deliver the word and leave it there.

This will help you; it will set you free. Otherwise, you'll live out of your emotions and become critical. Prophets who don't live by the spirit have a tendency to become critical, upset, and angry because they don't see what they're expecting to happen. This is another reason why emerging prophets need to be sit and be trained on the Prophet's Porch by seasoned Prophets.

How that by revelation He made known to me the mystery, as I have briefly written already, by which, when you read, you may understand my knowledge in the mystery of Christ. Which in other ages was not made known to the sons of men, as it has now been revealed by the Spirit to His holy apostles and prophets. Ephesians 3:3-5

Now, don't get upset if you're not a prophet or an apostle. If you're a pastor, teacher, or evangelist, don't be angry with them. They didn't decide this; God intended it this way. God made it so apostles and prophets would receive a revelation of things others did not see did or hear before. God gave this ability to apostles and prophets. There is an anointing upon prophets to see. There is a revelation by the Holy Spirit of things that were unknown for ages.

But to each one of us grace was given according to the measure of Christ's gift. Therefore, He says, 'When He ascended on high, He led captivity captive and gave gifts to men.'" Why did He give them? Why did He ascend and descend? Ephesians 4:10 says, "that he might fill all things. Ephesians 4:7

He gave prophets because there were some things that were not filled that needed to be filled.

And He gave some to be apostles, some prophets. Ephesians 4:11

Notice it says "some." That means not everyone is a prophet. Just because you prophesy doesn't mean you are a prophet. There's a difference between the gift of prophecy, the spirit of prophecy, and the ministry gift of a prophet. I have a course I teach about these 3 Dimensions of the Prophetic I teach in churches, and it's offered as an online course. Just like

11: The Prophet's Porch

there's a difference between someone who is an exhorter and an evangelist. You can preach, yet that doesn't make you an evangelist.

And He gave some to be prophets ... For the equipping of the saints, for the work of ministry, for the edifying of the body of Christ. Ephesians 4:11-12

Why do we need prophets?

He gave prophets to help equip and strengthen us. Prophets, like apostles, have a unique anointing for building the vision and the house of God. There are many who have extremes in their views about prophets. Some people get excited when a prophet visits the church, hoping to get a word and others are afraid. They believe prophets come into the church to expose things, so everyone feels the need to duck. They fear the prophet knows what they're thinking and will correct them. On the other hand, some people have the opposite view, thinking prophets only come to prophesy material blessings, like Jaguars and Cadillacs. A true prophet isn't just going to prophesy blessings, nor are they coming to point fingers in judgment. A true prophet comes to build and strengthen the church of God.

In the entire Bible, prophets are mentioned over 300 times, with 60 references in the New Testament alone! This tells us the importance of prophets. We need prophets. Without them, we have no spiritual profit.

Believe in the Lord your God, and you shall be established; believe His prophets, and you shall prosper." 2 Chronicles 20:20

The Prophet defined!

The Hebrew word "Nabi" means "one who speaks by inspiration" (Strong's 520). Another Hebrew word, "Kazow," refers to "a beholder of visions." The Greek word for prophet is "an interpreter, forthteller, and foreteller of the will of God." On the hand of God, prophets are represented by the pointing finger. One of the five "G"s of the prophetic is "guide." The face of an eagle represents the prophet, the air force of God's kingdom. The eagle is the king of the air.

A prophet is an oracle or spokesperson of God, able to foretell and forthtell the heart and mind of God for people, congregations, cities, regions, and nations. Christ Himself was recognized as a prophet. He referred to Himself as a prophet in Matthew 10:41, Matthew 13:57, and Luke 13:33. Others also referred to Him as a prophet, as seen in Matthew 21:11, John 4:18, John 6:14, and John 7:40.

First mention of a prophet!

Now, therefore, restore the man's wife, for he is a prophet. Genesis 20:7

This is the first time the term prophet is mentioned in the Bible. Prophets received visions, encounters, and proclaimed God's word in unusual ways. They performed symbolic actions like lying on their sides for days, wearing symbolic clothing, and confronting kings. Elijah, for example, called for rain and called down fire; these were acts performed by prophets.

In 1 Kings 17:1, prophets are described as those who stand before the Lord. While pastors have a ministry to stand before people, prophets primarily have a ministry to stand before the Lord. True prophets do more in private through prayer and intercession than they do publicly. They shift atmospheres and govern territories through their intercession. Jeremiah 27:18 shows prophets intercede for things to change. In Exodus 7:1-2, Aaron is raised up as a prophet for Moses.

Worship activates the Prophetic!

In 2 Kings 3:15-16, we see that worship activates the prophetic. They called for a minstrel, and then they prophesied. When true worship begins to flow, you'll begin to see healings, miracles, signs, wonders, and prophecy. In your church services and altar services where there's true worship, prophetic will flow. You find this in Revelation 19:10, "For the testimony of Jesus is the spirit of prophecy." When you worship God, you're testifying of Jesus. When you begin to lift Him up, He draws all men to Himself. In that spirit of worship, there's a spirit of prophecy.

11: The Prophet's Porch

People begin to flow in the gifts and the spirit of prophecy, and lives are changed.

The Hebrew root word for prophesy, "Naba," means "to bubble forth." Have you ever felt that? Have you ever felt something bubbling in your belly? Out of your belly shall flow rivers of living water. There's a bubbling up and a bubbling forth of the Word of God—the Naba flow. Just lift your hands and pray with and in the Holy Ghost. There's a bubbling forth; there's a Naba—a bubbling forth of the Word of God. Why? To equip, to edify, to bring to maturity, to bring to the knowledge of the Son of God. This is why God uses prophets to prophesy and to stir up His people to begin to prophesy as well.

Distinguishing the Difference

Now this man had four virgin daughters who prophesied. And as we stayed many days, a certain prophet named Agabus came down from Judea. Acts 21:9-11

Notice in this passage: you see four virgins who prophesied and a certain prophet. It's distinguishing the difference; you can prophesy, still that doesn't mean you're a prophet. The prophet moves with specificity, with pinpoint accuracy. You can read more about the functions of a prophet in 1 Corinthians 14:31 and 1 Corinthians 14:28-29.

1. **Prophets are essential in the local church.** The whole world just went through the covid pandemic. What is essential and non-essential? Who are the essential workers of this time, and who should be out of the house and who should stay at home, etc. We must not leave the prophets out. We need them in our lives and in the church more than ever before.

2. **Prophets help build and equip.** Ephesians 4:11-15; Ezra 5:2 says, "Then rose up Zerubbabel the son of Shealtiel, and Jeshua the son of Jozadak, and began to build." Notice this is Old Testament. What is it? The Old Testament is the New Testament concealed. The New Testament is the Old Testament revealed. We see prophets in the Old Testament were builders. "They

began to build the house of God, which is at Jerusalem, and with them were the prophets of God helping them." Prophets helped to build the house of God. Prophets should not be lone rangers. They need to be a part of the house of God.

3. **Prophets help complete the work.** *And the elders of the Jews built, and they prospered through the prophesying of Haggai the prophet and Zechariah the son of Iddo. And they built and finished it. Ezra 6:14* When you get around prophets, they help you build the house, they help you prosper, and they help you finish. Do you want to be part of something that's finished and done with excellence? That's what happens when you have prophets in your midst.

4. **Prophets prophesy with greater weight and authority. A. Prophets are not limited to the three primary areas of the gift of prophecy: to edify, to encourage, and to comfort.** A prophet's ministry goes beyond the basic functions of the gift of prophecy. Some people try to limit prophets to what is described in 1 Corinthians 12. However, that refers to the gift of prophecy, not the ministry gift of the prophet. There is a difference. A true prophet, when properly submitted to authority, can minister prophetically in areas of direction, correction, confirmation, impartation, activation, and demonstration.

5. **Prophets are eagles who soar into the heavens to see and hear the counsel of God and the plans of the enemy.** Once they have seen and heard, they deliver the word of the Lord to the apostles, who then decree and deploy the troops to carry it out on the earth.

You see, they are the air force of God. If prophets are given a platform in a church, if the pastor or leader is not insecure, the church will see prophets ascending into the heavens, returning to share what they see and hear. The church will prosper in the things of God. The church will grow, be built up, and be edified when prophets are active.

6. **When words of correction are necessary, they should always be given in love.** Ephesians 4:16 tells us to speak the truth in love. I've been around prophets who have become critical, likely

11: The Prophet's Porch

because they haven't spent enough time in their prayer closet. They may have been hurt by the church, and eventually, they begin to speak the truth, although in a way that cuts and hurts people. This is not the right approach. We need to speak the truth to build people up. Yes, some things need to be cut off, but it doesn't have to be done harshly.

7. **Prophets help establish the vision by prophesying, declaring, and proclaiming the vision in prayer.** Look at Habakkuk 2:1-3, Job 22:28, and Romans 4:17. Prophets prophesy, declare, and work to see the vision through. They don't let a word sit on a shelf or wait for a pulpit on Sunday. They change environments through prayer.

8. **Prophets help the apostle by tearing down and destroying the plans of the enemy.** You could also say they tear down strongholds in territories. Prophets confront the enemy's plans over the church, city, region, and nation.

9. **Prophets recognize their Metron:** Some prophets have greater measures of rule. The Bible talks about our measure of rule. The Apostle Paul said, "I will not boast beyond my measure of rule." The Greek word for this is "Metron." Each prophet has a Metron, a measure of rule. Years ago, when talking to Kim Clement, he wouldn't go to a particular area until he had authority to do so. He would minister in one location until the Lord opened another city for him. Many people engage in spiritual warfare over things they're not called to fight. Take it from someone who has some battle scars. If you saw me in the spirit, you'd see I'm a bit stronger there than in my physical body. You'd also see some cuts and wounds because I've learned some things the hard way. Stay within your grace, and when the Lord increases your measure of rule, then you can step out further. It's important for us to understand and operate in our measure of rule. If you're a prophet to a church, be happy and faithful in that church. If you're faithful with a little, God will make you ruler over much. If you try to go beyond your calling and act as a prophet to a city, region, or nation without the proper authority, you become an easy target for the enemy. Stay where you're graced.

Over time, as God increases your measure of rule, you can prophesy to larger territories.

10. **Prophets recognize and respect Protocol.**
A true prophet will recognize the authority in the church and follow its protocol to enhance the ministry. Each ministry has a different protocol, and prophets should submit to the leadership, whether they are in itinerant ministry or serving within a house. In-house prophets need to align with the leadership and follow the established protocols. Don't kick against it. If God wanted you to be in authority over that house, He would have set you there. He placed you under the vision to serve it.

Some people say, "I'm not under anybody other than God." That's the problem. If you can't come under authority and serve another's vision, God can never trust you with your own. Jesus said, *"If you're not faithful over another man's vineyard, you won't have your own."* Many are not called to have our own. It's often better to serve where you're called than to take on a weight you're not meant to carry. In America, there's an independent spirit. People leave to start their own thing and waste time when they could be building what God intended with someone else.

I have set watchmen on your walls, O Jerusalem; they shall never hold their peace, day or night. You who mention the Lord, do not keep silent, and give Him no rest till He establishes and till He makes Jerusalem praiseworthy throughout the earth. Isaiah 62:5-7

11. **Prophets are watchmen on the wall.**
They sound the alarm when the enemy tries to sneak into the church as a wolf in sheep's clothing. Prophets are like good sheepdogs, helping the shepherd defend the flock. Now, I'm not calling prophets dogs. But a true prophet will warn the sheep and protect them from the wolves.

Four ways to discern between true and false prophets.

You can read more about this in 1 John 4:1 and Jeremiah 5:30-31. These four questions should be asked about any of the Fivefold ministries:

11: The Prophet's Porch

1. **Do they glorify God?** Look at Deuteronomy 13:1-5, John 15:26, John 16:13-14, and Revelation 19:10. Does their ministry glorify God or themselves?

2. **How is their fruit?** When you look at the fruits of their family, finances, marriage, and relationships, what do you see? The Bible says, *"You shall know a tree by the fruit it bears."* A true prophet will walk in the fruit of the Spirit, not the fruit of the flesh. This applies to all Fivefold ministries. If you are a great preacher but are angry, mean, or hateful, you need deliverance. You need to be set free. If you can't be nice to your spouse, children, or others, you need to sit down and seek restoration. How can clean water and dirty water flow through the same stream? Let God deal with your heart.

   I'm talking about a Spirit-filled preacher. I was full of anger and hurt. You can't preach in that condition. The Lord healed me, but I went to a counselor, and I stayed with that counselor for months. I even took my kids to go to that counselor for months, and the Lord healed our family. He restored us. He restored my ability to believe and to have faith, and now He has blessed me with a beautiful wife and children. Now, I can preach not out of hurt, but to speak the truth in love. If you're hurting, if you're a prophet, if you're any leader — but especially if you're a prophet — seek healing. Don't speak out of anger or hurt. Speak the truth in love. Walk in the fruit of the Spirit.

3. **Is it biblical?** That's the third question to ask yourself when someone is ministering. Is what they're saying biblical? Rhema will never contradict Logos. You can find that in 2 Peter 1:20-21. Rhema will never contradict Logos. Sometimes people will say, "I had a vision. I had a dream. I had a word," nevertheless, if it's not biblical, you know what you should do with that? Cast it out.

   I've had people come over and lay hands on me without asking my permission. I'm careful about what I receive because I don't want anything contaminated coming to me or through me. When they're praying over me, this is what I do under my breath: "Lord, I receive anything that's of You, and anything that's not of You, I do not receive. I shut it down if it's not of God and I receive it if it's of God." That's what you must do. You must guard yourself. There are spiritual transmitted diseases (STDs). You must be careful.

You'll wonder why you're thinking or feeling a certain way; it might be because you sat under someone with that perversion and mess in them. Is it biblical? If someone is ministering to you and it's not biblical, cast the devil out. Cast it out. Throw it down. Cast down every imagination that exalts itself against the knowledge of God. If it's not the word of the Lord, pull it down. Don't receive it.

You must do this verbally. If you've heard it, you must verbally say, "I denounce that. I renounce it. I do not receive that in Jesus' name." I've had to be forceful at times. When people try to say something to me — family or whoever else — I say, "I don't receive that." They're like, "What? You don't receive that?" I tell them, "That is not the word of the Lord. I do not receive that." You don't have to be rude, still you must be firm. Over my family, I'll get in the car after being in a conversation with people and say, "That is not the word of the Lord. We do not receive that." I tell my family, "We do not receive that."

Otherwise, people will say to you, "You're mad" or "You're angry," or "You're sick" or "You're going to lose this," and you just sit there agreeing with it. No, I don't. The Lord tells me, "Don't even nod your head." I sit with people who want me to agree with them, not even nodding my head. That's what He does with me because I'm not going to receive something that's not of God.

4. **Are they willing to be judged?** This applies to every Fivefold ministry. In Scripture, one would prophesy, and another would

11: The Prophet's Porch

judge. Where did that go in the charismatic church? Why don't we judge a word anymore? Why do we let anything go? They were humble and submitted, and the Apostle Paul said, "Let one prophesy, let another judge." He wasn't saying you can only have two or three prophecies in a service. He was setting order.

When a word is given, the set man or woman, the leadership of the church, should come up and say, "This is the word of the Lord; we receive this." If it's not the word of the Lord, they should come up and correct it, either then or before the end of that service, and clarify the truth. They should take that person aside and say, "I love you, except that word was off." If they're a wolf, you might have to address it publicly, however, if they're learning, you guide them gently. Judge it.

If a prophet is not willing to be judged, they shouldn't have any place in your life or authority in your church. You should want to be judged. That's humility. That's how you should act when you're under authority. Not with an attitude of "I know it all." Let someone judge you. It's good.

I've stood before my church and repented. I brought all the prophets up and we repented before the congregation. We said, "We're sorry. We received words that were not of God, and we ask your forgiveness." Then, we went on a six-month fast from prophesying. During that time, the only way we would prophesy was if the Lord said so, and it would only be done by an elder or leader. After six months, the Lord said, "Make it another six months." It was the hardest time of our church, a yearlong fast from prophesying. Some people got mad and left the church, but our church became clean, based on love and purity from then on.

God does nothing without revealing it to the prophets.

Surely the Lord God does nothing unless He reveals His secret to His servants the prophets. Amos 3:7

Prophets are deeply involved in what God is doing. If something significant is happening in God's kingdom, prophets know about it. God reveals His plans to His prophets so they can declare it. They are His mouthpieces.

A lion roared! Who will not fear? The Lord God has spoken! Who can only prophesy? Amos 3:8

When the Lion, the apostle roars and takes dominion, the eagles, God's prophets and Air Force are able to soar and prophesy more freely.

That's why we need prophets. We need them in the church. In 1 Samuel 9, we see the "seer" anointing. The prophet Samuel prophesied over Saul, and Saul was turned into another man. His heart was changed, and he began to prophesy. When you get around prophets, you can't help but prophesy. You might not be a prophet, yet the spirit of prophecy will come upon you when you spend time with prophets. A true prophet doesn't just want you to listen to them; they want to activate you to release the word of the Lord for yourself. You see this in 2 Chronicles 29 and 30, and in 2 Chronicles 35:15. Then you begin to see the "Schools of Prophets" introduced. Schools of prophets? You mean you can go to school and be raised up and trained prophetically? Yes, schools of prophets. People would follow the prophet, learn, be trained, activated, and raised up by Samuel or by Elijah and Elisha. They were activated as prophets. Because they served prophets, the anointing that was on the prophet came upon them, activating them to function prophetically.

You might say, "I don't believe in that." Well, you haven't read about Elisha, have you? Elisha was the water boy. That's what they called him — the water boy. He tended to the needs and served Elijah. But because asked Elisha before he was taken up what he wanted because he served Elijah, And Elisha said, "I want a double portion of your spirit." Elijah responded, "You've asked a hard thing, but if you see me when I'm taken away, you'll receive it." In other words, "If you have eye-to-eye, face-to-face relationship with me, you'll receive a double portion of my spirit."

11: The Prophet's Porch

Sure enough, when Elijah was caught up by that chariot of fire, Elisha received that mantle and a double portion of Elijah's spirit.

Yes, he was activated, and the waterboy began to deliver living water and prophesy to people. If you know how to serve the prophets that God sends to your life, get ready; that anointing will be activated in you.

Declaration: "We declare, and we decree we receive the ministry gift of the prophet. We receive the prophetic anointing that You have for our lives to build Your kingdom and establish Your church. We declare and decree that we will go to the Prophet's Porch and learn to hear the voice of God for ourselves and others. We will not be hearers only; we will be doers of Your word, In Jesus name, Amen."

Joshua Fowler

12

The Evangelist's Porch

Let's spend some time on the Evangelist's Porch and discover the benefits of receiving evangelistic ministry and impartation.

> *And He Himself gave some to be apostles, some prophets, some evangelists, and some pastors and teachers, for the equipping of the saints for the work of ministry, for the edifying of the body of Christ, till we all come to the unity of the faith and of the knowledge of the Son of God, to a perfect man, to the measure of the stature of the fullness of Christ; Ephesians 4:11-13*

And He gave..." Who gave? Jesus gave. What did He give? Gifts. And those gifts include some apostles, some prophets, some evangelists, pastors, and teachers. So, we see some are given as evangelists.

Now, some traditions are good — prayer, spending time in the Word, coming to church, as He said, "Forsake not the assembling of yourselves together". But we need to operate from the truth of God's Word. There are some good traditions, however when you have a man-made tradition, it can make the word of God powerless. In Matthew 15:6, it says, "Then he need not honor his father or mother. Thus, you have made the commandment of God of no affect by your tradition."

The traditional evangelist is typically seen as a man or woman who, in most circles within the body of Christ that operates as an itinerant ministry gift. This person comes to a church and does a series of meetings, perhaps only one, but usually a series we've called revival for years. Some may call it a conference. Most evangelists are seen in this light. We look at these evangelists and see people like Jesse Duplantis, Billy Graham, who has gone to be with the Lord, or historical figures like Oral Roberts, Jack Coe, or William Branham. We would call them evangelists.

In fact, you can read books about the healing evangelists — the generals of the faith who went before us. But most of us have put this gift in a box, limiting it to just an itinerant speaker. Through our traditions and mindsets, we've defined an evangelist as someone who comes to a building and preaches as a guest of the pastor. But I don't believe just because you go from city to city and speak in a building for a pastor, it automatically makes you an evangelist.

Let me help you and set you free from this notion. Great men of God such as Leonard Ravenhill said most of the people we call evangelists today are not truly evangelists — they are exhorters. They are simply preachers. A ministry gift of an evangelist is vastly different from someone who is just an exhorter.

Now, we need exhorters, we need preachers, but an evangelist will not only preach to you or ask for souls to be saved when they preach. The true ministry gift of an evangelist will equip you to do the work of an evangelist. The anointing of a true evangelist will stir something within you, making you want to get up and win souls. You'll feel like you can't sit still — it's like fire shut up in your bones, and you've got to go out and preach the gospel because you're not ashamed of it. The gospel is the power of God unto salvation. So, an authentic evangelist will not only stir you up emotionally but will also equip you practically to evangelize your sphere of influence.

A true evangelist won't just preach a series of meetings or lead people to the Lord at the altar; they'll get out of the building with you and lead you into the harvest. You might feel scared, thinking, "I can't do this; I can't evangelize." But the evangelist will say, "It's okay, just come with me. I'll show you how." They won't just tell you — they'll teach you and walk with you through it. They might ask you, "What's your elevator pitch? What's your 60-second testimony?" If you had 60 seconds with someone, what could you say that would help them find their way to an eternity with the Lord? Before you know it, the thing that once scared you becomes

12: The Evangelist's Porch

second nature. You'll be able to stand in front of someone and say, "I once was lost, but now I'm found. I met a man named Jesus." Whether your testimony is He delivered you from drugs, restored your family, or something else, you'll realize a person with an experience is never at the mercy of someone with just an argument. You'll be able to make the gospel tangible.

Jesus, the evangelist, embodied this. He was the Word of God made flesh. He was the well sitting on the well when He spoke to the Samaritan woman, revealing her life, leading her into her calling and destiny. She became the first evangelist sent out to share the gospel. Why? Because Jesus did the work of an evangelist.

In fact, Jesus is the Evangelist. We're just His vessels. True evangelist are not just seeking platforms when they are mature in their gift. True evangelists don't mind getting their hands dirty. They'll get in the trenches and take the flock on spiritual scavenger hunts, finding treasure in hidden places in the city and teaching the church how to win souls. Proverbs 11:30 says, "He that wins souls is wise." So, if wisdom is winning souls, then the opposite must be true as well: Those who don't are foolish.

Truly mature believers bear much fruit that remains.

By this My Father is glorified, that you bear much fruit; so you will be My disciples. John 15:8

You did not choose Me, but I chose you and appointed you that you should go and bear fruit, and that your fruit should remain, that whatever you ask the Father in My name He may give you. John 15:16

He's glorified when your fruit remains. He wants you to bear fruit, win souls, and reproduce. He wants you to be a disciple who makes disciples. So, when you meet a true evangelist, you'll see the difference between them and someone with a traditional mind-set. We don't need evangelists just to preach to us to make us happy — we need them to show us how to break out of the church box and go get the harvest.

The word "evangelist" is mentioned three times in the Bible, so it's not mentioned a lot, although it's essential. You can find it in Ephesians 4, 2 Timothy 4:5, and Acts 21:8. While it's not mentioned often, the need for evangelists is great. I believe God's anointing is upon the church right now, and this ox-like anointing — the evangelist's anointing — is rising within the church like never before. Now that apostles and prophets have been reestablished, I believe the anointing is coming back upon evangelists, pastors, and teachers. They're being re-identified. Evangelists are recognizing they can flow prophetically, too. You haven't seen evangelism until you've seen prophetic evangelism. When the prophetic anointing comes upon an evangelist, you'll see divine harvest explosions in a territory, because they're not limited to just their own grace.

Now that we see the apostolic and prophetic anointing being thoroughly established in the church, evangelists are being re-identified, coming forth as prophetic and apostolic evangelists.

Christ, The Evangelist!

Christ is the ultimate evangelist, as seen in John 4. This is where Jesus, the well sitting on the well, encounters the Samaritan woman. He tells her the hour has come when those who worship Him must worship in spirit and truth. He moves in a prophetic anointing, revealing she had five husbands and the one she was with now was not her own. But Jesus didn't reject her. He said, "If you drink the water I give, you'll never thirst again. In fact, I'll put in you a well of living water that will spring up and flow out to others." Jesus began to function as both an evangelist and a prophet in that moment, raising up the Samaritan woman to go forth and share the gospel. Despite what many churches might think, she was the first evangelist He commissioned, and because of her, all Samaria heard the gospel.

Evangelist's bring Good News!

The Greek word for evangelist means "a bearer of good news." In the hand of God, it's the index finger — the one that reaches the farthest. Evangelists gather. The face of the evangelist we see in Ezekiel 1 is the face of an ox. Why the ox? Because it works hard for the harvest. It goes

12: The Evangelist's Porch

where others won't go, takes territory that hasn't been taken, plows the ground, prepares the harvest, and reaps the harvest.

Evangelists preach the gospel, which means "good news" or "glad tidings." The first mention of the term is in Acts 21:8. The law of first mention is important when interpreting Scripture, and you should always interpret Scripture with Scripture.

God will never give us a rhema word, which conflicts with the logos. It will always be confirmed in His Word. So, if someone comes around prophesying or having visions that can't be backed up by Scripture, then they just had bad pizza or barbecue the night before. A true word will always line up with the Word of God.

> *On the next day, we who were Paul's companions departed and came to Caesarea and entered the house of Philip, the evangelist, who was one of the seven, stayed with him. Acts 21:8*

How's your serve?

Now, if you go back and read Acts 6, you'll see Philip, one of the seven. You'll see he was first ordained as a deacon. He knew how to have a servant's heart. What is a deacon? One who tends tables, one who serves, one who ministers. Before he ever became this great healing evangelist, he knew how to take care of the needs of the flock and serve. In fact, these deacons were positioned to feed the widows, take care of the orphans, and handle ministry needs. So, his first ministry was born and bathed in servanthood.

Jesus came to serve, not to be served. Christ modeled this by washing His disciples 'feet. When the apostles started ministry, the first thing they did was follow His example. They had been serving, but they said, "Now we need to give ourselves to the word and prayer," and they raised up servants that would go and serve and meet the needs of the people. Because Philip took his role in the kingdom seriously, submitting to authority. God promoted him and raised him up as Philip, the evangelist. When you have a servant's heart, God can trust you with greater things, with deeper things. Some might say, "Well, I did that in my last church. I did that back in 1995. I'm more mature than that." No, you never outgrow being a servant. In fact, Jesus said, "The least among you is the greatest, and the greatest among you is a servant." Your maturity is expressed through your servanthood. In fact, can I ask you today: How's your serve? When you watch a volleyball or tennis match, it's all in the serve. If your serve isn't right, you'll lose the match. And that's how it is in life. If you come to church and all you do is eat, eat, eat—"Give me, give me, give me. Pray for me, give me a word" — except you're not willing to serve, then you're just a cloud without rain. You're a cistern that receives but doesn't overflow. But when you serve, when you get planted and rooted in a house, and you let it flow, then it will increase. You'll be like Philip — the evangelist.

In Acts 8:4-8, you can see Philip healed people. People were delivered from demons, and others were freed from sicknesses and diseases. Philip flowed in the supernatural. You'll see in verses 12-13 and verses 26-40 how Christ moved through Philip. You'll see the good news coming out of him. You'll see the kingdom being preached by Philip in verse 35, and in verse 40, you'll see the name of Jesus being preached by Philip. He wasn't just preaching the gospel of salvation. An evangelist preaches and equips people in the kingdom.

Functions of an Evangelist

1. **Edification**: They help edify the church.
2. **Proclamation**: They proclaim the good news.
3. **Infiltration**: They go, train, and lead others to gather the harvest.

12: The Evangelist's Porch

Evangelists: The Marines of The Kingdom of God!

If you were to compare the ministry gift of an evangelist to someone in the military, I believe they are the Marines of The Kingdom of God! Evangelists are a lot like the marines. They infiltrate and go into places others might not go. They are always ready to go and take over. They are willing to go the extra mile. Have you ever been around a marine? I have friends who are marines, they say, "Once a marine, always a marine." Always ready to serve—that's an evangelist. They're the most intense people you'll ever be around. I should know—I was raised by one. My dad is an evangelist. You haven't seen someone intense until you meet my dad. He's a ball of fire. "Hoorah," he's ready to go and take over.

When you get around marines, they're like, "Where's the fight? Let me get in the face of it. Let me go in first." We need marines in the kingdom! We need evangelists. We need a fresh anointing to come upon the church and more evangelists to rise with this ox anointing and help us gather the harvest. They train and lead others to gather the harvest. This is the work of an evangelist.

Demonstration: You'll often see evangelists function and flow in words of knowledge and healing. These are two primary gifts they operate in, although they're not confined to them. When you're around an evangelist, you'll see words of knowledge being called out and people being healed. I believe we need some power evangelists to arise and help the church engage in power evangelism.

Impartation: Evangelists equip the saints for the work of the ministry. They don't just talk about it — they get you involved. Nike didn't come up with "Just Do It" — heaven did! Don't just be a hearer of the word; be a doer. When you're around an evangelist, they ask, "Why aren't you doing it? Get up, come on, let's go!" Evangelists get frustrated when they're in places where people just sit like bobbleheads. They've got the James Brown anointing—"Get on up!" They're ready for believers to get up and do something.

> *"For the equipping of the saints for the work of ministry, to the building up of the body of Christ." Ephesians 4:12*

All five gifts do this, but evangelists do it with the grace of gathering. They want to build you up, equip you, and then say, "Let's go get them. Let's go get those people held by hell. Let's go storm the gates of hell!" Evangelists are hell fighters. They have that ox anointing, helping us gather the harvest. They say, "Let's go get them!" Someone has your son, daughter, friend, or neighbor — they're being held captive, and the evangelist says, "We can't sit here until we die. Let's go get them!" They have that Holy Ghost hell-fighter anointing, snatching the lost out of the fire.

> *"but others save with fear, pulling them out of the fire, hating even the garment defiled by the flesh." Jude 23*

When you get around an evangelist, you will start thinking and acting like one. Next thing you will say, "I can do that." Then before you know it you too will do the work of an evangelist. Something stirs up within you—a courage to go and win the lost. Modern-day examples of evangelists include Reinhard Bonnke, Steve Hill, Todd White, Joe Oden, Levi Lutz and Nathan Morris. It's amazing to see how these gifts have grown. Bonnke started schools of evangelism, and now Daniel Kolenda is carrying that on through Christ for All Nations (CfaN). They're training evangelists, not just doing the work themselves. Bonnke transitioned to doing 90-day schools of evangelism, and friends of mine relocated to be trained and sent out. Todd White is also training people, showing them how to live a lifestyle of evangelism.

Longevity: Why do we need evangelists? Because we need longevity. We need a harvest. If you only keep the people who are already saved in this building, eventually you'll dwindle, just like some denominations today. They're closing 3 or 4 churches and combining them because there's no growth. Growth and longevity come through evangelism.

The False Evangelist:

I marvel that you are turning away so soon from Him who called you in the grace of Christ to <u>a different gospel.</u> Which is not another, but there are some who trouble you and want to <u>pervert the gospel of Christ</u>. But even if we, or an angel from heaven, preach any other gospel to you than what we have preached to you, let him be accursed. As we have said before, so now I say again, if anyone preaches any other gospel to you than what you have received, let him be accursed. For do I now persuade men or God? Or do I seek to please men? For if I still pleased men, I would not be a bond servant of Christ. Galatians 1:6-10

False evangelists are man-pleasers. They preach another gospel to tickle the ears of their listeners and build crowds. False evangelists want you to follow them instead of following Christ.

Here's the difference: We all must ask ourselves, Am I glorifying God, or glorifying myself? With social media being what it is today, we must make sure we keep Jesus at the center and not our ministries and signs and wonders. We need to preach Jesus, not ourselves and our ministries. We don't need to preach another gospel. When you're around a true evangelist, your heart will burn for Jesus. After sitting under a true evangelist, you'll be more in love with Jesus than before! You'll be a follower of Jesus, and you'll want to make more followers of Jesus.

Declaration: "We declare and decree that we receive the ministry gift of the Evangelist. We receive the evangelistic anointing that You have for our lives to build Your kingdom and establish Your church. We will be equipped on to the Evangelist's Porch and help gather in the harvest. We will not be hearers only; we will be doers of Your word. In Jesus name, Amen"

Joshua Fowler

13

The Pastor's Porch

Let's spend some time on the Pastor's Porch and discover the benefits of receiving pastoral ministry and impartation.

And He Himself gave some to be apostles, some prophets, some evangelists, and some pastors and teachers, for the equipping of the saints for the work of ministry, for the edifying of the body of Christ, till we all come to the unity of the faith and of the knowledge of the Son of God, to a perfect man, to the measure of the stature of the fullness of Christ; Ephesians 4:11-13

But to each one of us grace was given according to the measure of Christ's gift. Therefore, He says, When He ascended on high, He led captivity captive and gave gifts to men. Now this, 'He ascended'— what does it mean other than He also first descended into the lower parts of the earth? He who descended is also the one who ascended far above all the heavens, that He might fill all things. Ephesians 4:7-8

Fill All things!

Why did He descend and why did He ascend? That He might fill all things. Get that in your spirit. Verse 11: "And He gave some to be apostles, some prophets, some evangelists, and some pastors and teachers." The NASB translation, as we mentioned earlier, says, "some as apostles, some as prophets." Verse 12: "For the equipping of the saints." Why did He give pastors? For the equipping of the saints, for the work of ministry.

He is equipping the church to do the work. We don't go to church and say, "Pastor, Pastor, we need you to do this for us. Oh, Pastor, can you get me some water? I need a bottle. I need a pacifier." No, God gives pastors to teach us to do the work of the ministry. This is truth versus tradition.

You've got to get this in your spirit, or as Dr. Larry Lee used to say, "You've got to know it in your knower." Know it deep in your spirit. You need to understand what the enemy has done for years — he has plundered the church. He robbed the church. He has misidentified what a pastor is. If you have the wrong identity, you'll end up with the wrong destiny. You must have the right identity to move into your destiny.

> *Thus you have made the commandment of God of no affect by your tradition. Matthew 15:6*

You've made the Word of God of no affect by your tradition. Traditions have limited the ministry gift of pastor. Traditions have boxed the gift of pastor in and made it something vastly different than what God designed it to be. Much of our western church culture has shrouded the true gift of pastor. Once we see the authentic gift of a pastor biblically, we are able to unearth and receive the depth of this gift.

During the Dark Ages, we lost much of this understanding. We lost the flow of the gifts of the Spirit. We lost the knowledge of the Word for ourselves. The Word was relegated only to the clergy and taken away from the church, so the congregation couldn't read the Word for themselves. So, they couldn't check anything against Scripture. We lost the understanding "the just shall live by faith." That had to be restored with Martin Luther when he nailed the 95 Theses to the door, declaring, "We're not going to buy our way into heaven. We're not buying our way out of purgatory or hell. The Just shall live by faith."

Since the Protestant Reformation, we've been on the road to recovery. We've been recovering the Ark — we've been like "raiders of the lost Ark." We have been restoring the Ark of God, the Presence of God, the covenant of God, the plan of God, and the Word of God. And now, we're seeing what a pastor is truly meant to be.

In Catholicism, in the Roman Catholic Church, we moved away from pastors and replaced them with priests. We did away with apostles and instead focused on priests or reverends. In the Catholic Church, we

13: The Pastor's Porch

replaced pastors, apostles, prophets, evangelists, and teachers with bishops, cardinals and popes—big fish hats, big robes, and very little anointing. Big titles, "kiss my ring," and the mentality "I know the Word, you don't — you're a peasant." But God has been restoring His church. For years, people looked to the Pope, and some still do. But many others looked to the Pope or the priest, feeling they had to go into a confessional booth to get their sins forgiven and be told to say a certain number of Hail Marys. That system had to be demolished to restore the truth "The Just shall live by faith." We don't need to go to someone else to pray and say a certain number of Hail Marys. We can go directly to the Father through the Son, Jesus Christ. We can boldly approach His throne.

You might ask, "What does this have to do with pastors?" Because if we're not careful, we'll take our ideology of priests, popes, and bishops, and simply transfer that understanding over to another man with the title "pastor." We'll elevate him over everything in the church and fail to recognize he is just one of five, and we need all five. It was easy during the Protestant Reformation to move from an understanding of priests to reverends, clergy, ministers, and pastors. "Oh, Pastor, you're going to take care of me. You're going to change our diapers. You're going to give us a bottle. You're going to give us a pacifier." If you look at most pastors in America, if you opened their jackets, they'd be full of pacifiers. "You want one? Here's another one for you, and here's another one for you." We've turned pastors into something they were never ordained to be. Pastors are called to help equip the saints. Yes, pastors are called to edify, to build up the church. Pastors are called to help you and I come to the stature of Christ. They're not called to baby us, pacify us, or coddle us. Pastors are called to help us become mature believers.

Now, pastors do carry a shepherd's heart, however a true shepherd isn't just someone who coddles us when there's a wolf coming.

You'll recognize a shepherd by watching him tend to his flock. He will defend and protect them. There is a warrior's heart in the shepherd. Look at David. He was not just a little shepherd boy; he would take out Goliath.

He would take out the bear and the lion. So, pastors are not just called to be meek, timid, or shy, nor to just hand out pacifiers. I'm breaking down these traditions because America has made God in our own image. God said, "Let us make man in our image," but we've turned it around in the church and made God in our image. We've shaped pastors into what we want them to be. "Pastor, you have to be at everything we have. You don't have a family. We don't want to learn to pray for ourselves. You have to come and pray for us."

But that's not what the Bible says. The Bible says if you have a need, call for the elders of the church. It didn't say to call just the pastor. He's just one of the elders. But if the pastor isn't at your ball game, recital, or at your bedside in the hospital, some people say, "I'm not going to that church anymore. That pastor doesn't care about me." No, a true church that's Fivefold will raise up elders — plural — and then you call for the elders, not just the pastor. Now, one of the elders might be a pastor, only we must be delivered from needing a man and instead receive God's hand. If we're not careful, we'll be fixated on the headman or woman of the church and won't receive the fullness of God's hand: apostles, prophets, evangelists, pastors, and teachers.

Redefining the Gift of The Pastor!

The term "pastor" is referred to 1 time in the New Testament. Isn't that amazing? In Ephesians 4:11, you see the Greek word "Poimen," which is used 18 times in the New Testament, but is only translated as "pastor" once. So, it means to tend sheep by watching over them as an associate, close friend, and companion—to keep company, fellowship, and feed. The shepherding heart is to tend to the flock. As I said earlier, it's represented by the ring finger — shepherds are married to the church, in covenant with God's house. It's the face of a man, the one that represents humanity to God and God to humanity. There's a representation of humanity among the sheep. A shepherd smells like sheep.

You go to some churches where they call the leader a shepherd or a pastor, yet he doesn't know the flock. He's whisked in and whisked out, has a lot

13: The Pastor's Porch

of armor bearers, and doesn't know anybody. He doesn't smell like the sheep. You know what he is? At worst, he's a hireling. At best, he's an exhorter or has lost his way in the systems of men. But, He is not a true shepherd or pastor.

Shepherds, pastors, are among the people. That doesn't mean they don't have their own lives, or they are the only ones who jump to meet every need. But if you're around a true shepherd, a real pastor, they smell like the sheep. They know their sheep. They tend to them. The "G" in the 5G for pastor stands for "guards." The pastor guards the flock. Pastors protect the flock from wolves in sheep's clothing.

Rediscover, Re-identify and Reemphasize

I believe this is a time of rediscovery, re-identification and a reemphasis on the ministry gift of the authentic pastor. The real deal, Pastor. What a real pastor is being unearthed from the religious debris and traditional mindsets of men. The authentic pastor is being re-identified. I believe pastors, evangelists, and teachers will now really come into their true identities, now that the apostles and prophets have been restored. The pastor, evangelist, and teacher will begin to move and flow in dimensions they've never moved in before. More true shepherds and pastors will begin to arise than we've ever seen. I'm not referring to Saul's religious regime — kings hiding in tents or green rooms afraid to engage in warfare for the people. I'm talking about Davids who've trained on the backside of the desert, who tended the sheep, played songs when nobody was there, worshiped, and defended the sheep. They've killed the bear and the lion, and when they see a Goliath coming against their church, their God, or their nation, these Davids, these singing shepherds, will arise as true shepherds and defend the flock. They'll defend the city. They'll say, "Not in this city! I've been called to be a shepherd in this city. You're not bringing that doctrine of devils into this city, this region, or this nation."

True shepherds are rising. True Davids. These Davids are worshipers. These Davids are warriors. They know how to war. They know how to intercede. They know how to pray. They know what it means to live lives in obscurity, unknown and hidden. They're not worried about their title, their name, their rank, or their position. They're only concerned about tending to the sheep God has given them. True shepherds.

JESUS, The Good, Great & Chief Shepherd!

"And when the Chief Shepherd appears, you will receive the crown of glory that does not fade away." 1 Peter 5:4

May the God of peace who brought up our Lord Jesus from the dead. Jesus, that great Shepherd of the sheep, through the blood of the everlasting covenant, make you complete in every good work to do His will. Working in you what is well-pleasing in His sight, through Jesus Christ, to whom be glory forever and ever. Amen. Hebrews 13:20

I am the Good Shepherd. The Good Shepherd gives His life for the sheep. John 10:11

This shows you the good and great Shepherd, our Lord and Savior, Jesus Christ. I believe we're going to get a greater revelation and impartation from the Shepherd in this season.

Psalm 23—most of us have memorized this passage. This might be one of the first passages you memorized as a little girl or boy. I remember my mom teaching me that, and then through the Psalms, I remember Psalm 23. It just runs in my spirit.

The Lord is my shepherd; I shall not want. He makes me to lie down in green pastures; He leads me beside the still waters. He restores my soul; He leads me in the paths of righteousness for His name's sake. Yea, though I walk through the valley of the shadow of death, I will fear no evil; for You are with me; Your rod and Your staff, they comfort me. You prepare a table before me in the presence of my enemies; You anoint my head with oil; my cup runs over. Surely goodness and mercy shall follow me all the days of my life, and I will dwell in the house of the Lord forever. Psalm 23:1-6

13: The Pastor's Porch

I want you to know Jesus is your Shepherd. He's your provider, your protector. He's modeled this in Scripture, so the shepherds that God is raising up will act like the Good Shepherd. We are to follow His lead.

> *For unto us a Child is born, unto us a Son is given; and the government will be upon His shoulder. And His name will be called Wonderful, Counselor, Mighty God, Everlasting Father, Prince of Peace. Of the increase of His government and peace there will be no end. Upon the throne of David and over His kingdom, to order it and establish it with judgment and justice from that time forward, even forever. The zeal of the Lord of hosts will perform this. Isaiah 9:6*

If you go on to read the verses before that, you'll see He is the One who was broken, bruised, and gave His life for His flock. By His stripes, we are healed.

Jesus is our Model!

This is the Defender we have. This is the Protector we have. This is the Counselor we have. This is the Redeemer we have. This is the Friend we have. And this is how shepherds are to live their lives. They need to follow the Good Shepherd. Not as untouchables — we've had too many pretenders and not enough pastors. People who can preach, however, are more like celebrity Christians than servant leaders. God is changing that. He's raising up Davids and removing Sauls. He's removing the pharaohs who have turned churches into controlled concentration camps and holding tanks. He's raising up shepherds who will work with all the Fivefold ministries to equip the saints and send them out to do the work of the ministry. He's raising up shepherds who don't have inferiority complexes, who aren't guarding their pulpits or hogging the platform. They want to raise up others to teach, preach, prophesy. True shepherds who want to equip the saints to do the work of the ministry.

The First Mention

Shepherds are first mentioned in Genesis 46:31-34. If you get a chance, go there and read it. You'll also read about shepherds in Ezekiel 34:11-16.

We've already mentioned Psalm 23. Isaiah 40:11, Jeremiah 23:4, and Amos 3:12 also admonish us through the Word of God, showing what a true shepherd is and what a false shepherd is. If shepherds try to become saviors, they'll miss the mark. When a shepherd thinks he can meet all the needs of the flock and doesn't lead the people to the Good Shepherd, he's acting like a Catholic priest, standing between the people and God. Catholicism is a broken religion. You don't need to be a priest to stand between the people and God. You need to be a shepherd who leads them to the Good Shepherd.

What proves a shepherd's heart?

A true shepherd will flow in words of wisdom, words of knowledge, and the gifts of healing, because they have a heart to pick up sheep that are broken and minister to their needs. You will see the gifts of the Spirit flow through a shepherd. They're not limited, as tradition has taught us, to just speaking in church and administrating business. We have attempted to confine pastors into being glorified baby sitters and church administrators, but they are much more than that. They can flow in the supernatural. There's an impartation that comes from shepherds. What is their impartation? They equip and edify so you can do the work of the ministry. If you get around a true shepherd, you'll develop a shepherd's heart. You'll want to smell like sheep too. You'll want to hang out with the people. You won't think you're better than anyone else. You won't be untouchable. You'll know you're a servant and want to serve.

Cross-training and Cross-pollination

People come to church and say, "Well, I don't want to serve in the youth or children's department. I don't want to do this, or I don't want to do that. I'm called to be a prophet." No, if you can't minister to the people's needs, then you don't need to have a microphone and prophesy. The best thing that can happen to a prophet is to learn to tend to the sheep. When a prophet gets balanced and develops a shepherd's heart, then he or she will prophesy out of love, not with a critical spirit. So, you want to receive that shepherd's heart. If you are a pastor, you want to receive the prophetic anointing so you can pastor prophetically. You want to have cross-training from one another — cross-pollination — so we can grow and come into the fullness of Christ.

In summary, we need true shepherds to help feed, heal, and guard us. They do much more than that, however, these are three of the primary traits of true shepherds: they feed, heal, and guard.

WARNING: Sacred Cow Tipping!

Now, I'm going to say something that might upset some people if they're holding onto a sacred cow. I'm going sacred cow tipping here. This might rock your boat. Here's your religious warning: Religious spirits might be offended by what I'm about to say. Pastors are not called to have a relationship with God for you. They're called to lead you to have a relationship with God for yourself. If a shepherd is worth his or her salt, if they do their job well, they will lead you to the Good Shepherd, and you will have your own relationship with God. You'll be better off — you won't be codependent. When a shepherd doesn't do his job well, you will become dependent, codependent on them for everything. A true shepherd doesn't have a savior complex. He will back up and say, "No, you need to hear God for yourself. You need to know God for yourself." He'll give you that tough answer in a crisis.

Real shepherds, many of them, do not lead the church. Many shepherds are within the congregation. They may be an elder or a deacon, but they might never preach. Their pulpits might be their coffee-tables or their dinner tables. True shepherds are among the sheep, tending to the sheep. Maybe they're under someone who's called a pastor, or maybe they're under someone else in the Fivefold ministry, but they are part of the Fivefold, functioning within the house, within the body, shepherding the flock. And they don't have to tear away their little group to go start another church and put their banner up. They can be a shepherd, be submitted to authority, and function in a church without needing to be the head.

In fact, that was the way the early church functioned. Nowhere in the New Testament will you find the word "pastor" as the head of a church. Now, I'm not saying you can't have a pastor leading a church — I believe any of the Fivefold ministries can be raised up by God and set as the Lead Elder or Bishop of a church. However, we've inherited a Catholic mind-set where the roles of priest, pope, and pastor have merged. We tend to call anyone who oversees a church "pastor," but that's not biblically accurate. In fact it seems like in many of our congregations anyone who is designated as a leader it called pastor. We have Lead Pastors, Senior Pastors, Associate Pastors, Bus Pastors, Children's Pastors, Youth Pastors, Worship Pastors, College & Career Pastors, Media Pastors, Campus Pastors, Parking Lot Pastors, everyone is a pastor. I believe this has limited the growth spiritually and numerically within much of the church. It's confusing for those who are called to fulfill other ministry gift callings because we have limited them to only one gift. Otherwise they are relegated to itinerate ministry as evangelists or to the mission field as a missionary. I believe this must change to see the Greater Glory we've been praying for.

In the early church, if you read through Acts, you'll see it was the apostles and the elders who led. It was the apostles and the elders. In Antioch, you'll find the teachers and the prophets, and from there, they raised up and sent out Apostle Paul and Barnabas (Acts 13).

So, you don't even see the term "pastor" as the leader of the church government. Think of it as a 3x5 card. Does anybody remember those? We don't use paper as much in schools anymore with computers and iPads taking over, but we used to have 3x5 cards. Did you ever get one? This little card represents the government of the church. If you ever want to know what church government looks like, think 3x5. The government of the church is simple: set man or set woman, elders, and deacons. That's the three-fold government of a church. I'll be teaching more on this in an upcoming session, probably in March. So, 3x5: set man, set woman, elders, and deacons — that's government in the church. The grace gifts include all five of the Fivefold ministries. And elders and deacons can be

13: The Pastor's Porch

any of the Fivefold ministry gifts under the set man or woman who has been ordained and commissioned to lead that flock. That person can be any of the five, raised up and appointed apostolically to do so.

So, God takes the Fivefold ministries and moves them into three offices. Offices represent government. There are only three offices in the church: the set man or woman (the Chief Elder / Bishop), elders, and deacons. Those are the offices of a church. So, if an apostle, prophet, evangelist, pastor, or teacher comes in from another place, they must submit to the deacons and elders of the church. They don't come in and oversee them. So, if you have Prophet So-and-So trying to come in and give a word but he's out of order, and a deacon says, "Sit down," he better sit down and respect that authority.

So throughout the New Testament, apostles, elders and deacons worked together. The elders and deacons were comprised of apostles, prophets evangelists, pastors and teachers working together and that's how the church grew. The Bible says, "The Lord added to the church daily such as should be saved" Acts 2:4, 47 and "The number of the disciples multiplied" in Acts 6:1,7. You don't have to become "the pastor" of your own church one day to be a pastor — you can pastor right where you're at among the flock. As you receive the impartation on the Pastor's Porch you will arise in maturity and help shepherd those in your sphere of influence.

Declaration: "We declare and decree that we receive the ministry gift of the Pastor. We receive the pastoral anointing that You have for our lives to build Your kingdom and establish Your church. We will help shepherd and care for those you put in our spheres of influence. We will receive all that you have for us on the Pastor's Porch and bring other with us also. We will not be hearers only; we will be doers of Your word. In Jesus name, Amen"

Joshua Fowler

14

The Teacher's Porch

Let's spend some time on the Teacher's Porch and discover the benefits of receiving the teacher's ministry and impartation. As I mentioned earlier, as a teenager, I grew up in a church where we had Sunday schoolteachers and schoolteachers, however I do not recall anyone recognizing among us the gift of a teacher. I was only accustomed to pastors and evangelists. The ministry gift of a teacher is essential for our personal and corporate spiritual growth. I know there has been a great emphasis on apostles and prophets over the last two or three decades, however we also really need to understand and receive teachers who can help bring us into maturity.

> *But to each one of us, grace was given according to the measure of Christ's gift. Therefore, He says: 'When He ascended on high, He led captivity captive and gave gifts to men. '(Now this, 'He ascended'—what does it mean but He also first descended into the lower parts of the earth? He who descended is also the One who ascended far above all the heavens, that He might fill all things.) And He gave some to be apostles, some prophets, some evangelists, and some pastors and teachers. For the equipping of the saints for the work of ministry, for the edifying of the body of Christ, till we come to the unity of the faith. And of the knowledge of the Son of God, to a perfect man, to the measure of the stature of the fullness of Christ. That we should no longer be children, tossed to and fro and carried about with every wind of doctrine, by the trickery of men. In the cunning craftiness of deceitful plotting. But speaking the truth in love. May grow up in all things into Him. He who is the head — Christ — from whom the whole body, joined and knit together by what every joint supplies, according to the effective*

working by which every part does its share. Causing growth of the body for the edifying of itself in love. Ephesians 4:7-14

Understanding what a True Teacher is!

When we receive the teaching gift — this part of the hand, the pinky — we are being grounded. What does the teacher do? The teacher grounds us in truth, helps us to be rooted and grounded in love, and in the Word. Teachers help us move into an understanding of the truth. "You shall know the truth, and the truth shall make you free"? So, it's not just hearing the truth; it's knowing and applying the truth. A teacher helps us know how to do this. I once heard it said this way: A preacher proclaims a thing, but a teacher explains the thing. A teacher brings an explanation of what we're receiving.

So, you can have a prophet come and proclaim something, prophesy something, declare it. But then a teacher can take that prophetic word, dig into the roots and truth of the word, and ground the people in that word. So, no longer are we just thinking, "Wow, we got a prophecy, we got a word," but now a teacher can say, "Okay, I'm glad we got that word. What does it mean? How do we apply it? How do we receive it? How do we act on it?" That's why we need teachers.

The 3x5 Card of The Kingdom!

Now, teachers are part of what I call the government of God in the church. They're part of it. I mentioned the 3x5 card earlier, didn't I? I'm glad you asked. So, you have three offices: the set man or woman over the church, the elders, and the deacons. I'll come back and teach more about that, but I also want to show you that there's a governmental grace upon three gifts: apostles, prophets, and teachers. Apostles, prophets, and teachers — there's a governmental grace upon them. You might ask, "How do you know that?"

And God has appointed these in the church: first apostles, second prophets, third teachers. 1 Corinthians 12:28

14: The Teacher's Porch

Where did He appoint them? In the church. The King James Version says, "And God hath set some in the church, first apostles," secondarily prophets, thirdly teachers. So, He appointed them in the church. He set them in the church. There's a governmental order in the church: apostles, prophets, and teachers. You'll see in Acts — prophets, teachers, and apostles. In Acts, we see apostles, prophets, and teachers such as Paul, Barnabas and Apollos flowing in the church. We also see Evangelists such as Phillip and Stephen flowing with the apostles, prophets and teachers. And although no-one named was ever referred to as a pastor in the New Testament, we know they were functioning in the church.

The Fivefold ministries function together. Apostles and Prophets are part of the foundation. Teachers help explain what the apostles and prophets are proclaiming, helping us get rooted and grounded in truth.

What is a Teacher?

So the pinky brings balance. "Didaskalos" means teacher and is also translated as master. A Teacher is one who comes with a now word of logos for the wounded spirit. So, a teacher doesn't just teach something from their head — it should not be head knowledge. It should be spirit knowledge.

There is a vast difference between a school teacher or a Sunday School teacher and the ministry gift of a teacher. The True Ministry Gift of Teacher functions with an anointing. When they come under that prophetic anointing, they begin to teach prophetically. There's a difference between a prophetic teacher and a teacher. Dad Samples would come to us and teach for three hours, and we'd want more in one night in a regular service. He would teach, and then in the middle of his teaching, he'd prophesy to somebody. Then go back to teaching some more. A little later, he'd see somebody healed, then go back and teach some more. I'd go up to him afterward, and he'd have just a few lines, and a few little things scribbled on a paper, and I would say, "Dad Samples, how do you do that?" He said, "Well, the Lord told me not to prepare a sermon, just to prepare my heart." He said, "I prepare my heart and write down a few things before I get up before the people to jog my memory. I just teach and share what the Lord said." This changed my life and ministry. I started moving away from just being locked into my notes.

A true teacher doesn't just give you head knowledge; they want to speak to your spirit. They want to equip you. I want to equip your spirit man, your inner man, to make you strong, to make you mature in the things of God.

Historically, Bible teachers and teachers were synonymous. If you look through America, the greatest universities — Yale, Harvard, Princeton — were all started as Bible colleges. These were teachers, teachers from the church who taught from the Bible. Our law came from the law of God's Word being taught. So, we must understand God wants anointed teachers in every part of society.

The teacher is mentioned roughly 40 times in the New Testament. Now, it was mentioned more than this. In fact, Jesus was referred to or alluded to as master, as rabbi, as teacher, 60 out of 90 times in the New Testament. But 40 times, you can find the teacher as a ministry gift mentioned. It is an ascension gift. This ministry gift was mentioned more than the others in the New Testament. Jesus was referred to more as a teacher, as a rabbi, as a master than He was referred to as anything. Partially because of where He was at—historically, people followed a rabbi, followed a master. But a lot of it was also because He showed Himself as a teacher. How many are thankful Jesus is the teacher? So, He taught the Word. He broke it down. He didn't just preach sermons. He gave the depth of the Word, and when He would pull away from sharing in parables with the masses, He would teach His disciples.

His teaching ministry was not just for a pulpit; it was a lifestyle. I want you to get that in your spirit. If you're around a true teacher, it's not just about what they do when they're in the pulpit in the church. Their life should be teaching, equipping, and raising people up.

14: The Teacher's Porch

Coming out of the corner!

"And though the Lord gives you the bread of adversity and the water of affliction, yet your teachers will not be moved into a corner anymore, But your eyes shall see your teachers." Isaiah 30:20

Your teachers will not be moved into a corner anymore. We need our teachers to get out of the corner and start teaching the truth. No more pushing them into a corner. The enemy wants to put a teacher in the corner. Anybody grow up in school and get put in the corner? They used to put a dunce cap on you and set you in the corner or hit you on the hand with a ruler. The enemy's been trying to take the teachers and put them in a corner. The enemy is trying to keep them from teaching the truth. The enemy wants us to exchange the truth of God's Word for Celebrity Christianity and. Many with itching ears and heaping unto themselves teachers with itching ears a spirit-lite, pop gospel. But I have good news, genuine, anointed teachers are arising with true revelation that grounds and matures believers.

A New Breed of Teachers Arising!

There's a new breed of teacher arising. There're some teachers coming up in this hour who have been hidden. Who are going to be revealed, and they're going to ground us in the truth of God's Word like we've never been grounded before. We've got to be careful. There's a great falling away, with people trying to lead others astray. Ephesians 4 shares with us the importance of receiving the Fivefold, so we're not an easy mark for the enemy, so we're not led astray by every wind of doctrine.

I believe the teaching gift is necessary — probably more so now than ever — to keep us from being led astray. People come as wolves in sheep's clothing, teaching another gospel, preaching something based on their own opinion. You know what? All of us have opinions. They're like armpits—they all stink. We don't need opinions; we need the truth of God's Word. We need God's truth. It's the truth that sets us free. It's the truth we know and apply that sets us free. We need to be grounded in the truth of God's Word. Teachers ground us. Teachers balance us. So, if we get all excited prophetically, they'll say, "Hey, wait. It's great. I'm glad you're excited. Now, what are we going to do with that word? How are we going to apply that word? Are we just going to put it in a little book and place it on the shelf and one day wait for it to happen?" No! We need to get that word—what does that word mean, and how can we activate it?

Teachers are not adamantly opposed to prophets; they are joined together. They are two sides of the same coin. You need that prophetic gift, and when a true teaching gift operates under a prophetic anointing, it becomes powerful. Similarly, when a true prophet submits to and understands a teaching anointing, and receives that explanation while embracing the teaching grace, the prophetic ministry goes to another dimension. I've seen it happen. On the other hand, when a teacher lacks prophetic grace, their teaching can become boring, making you feel like you need toothpicks to keep your eyes open and stay awake. But when that same teacher, with the same content, is anointed and flows prophetically, and says, "Okay, this is what I prepared, but Holy Spirit, say whatever you want to say," the teaching transforms. It speaks directly to the hearts of the people.

We need the teaching grace. Look at verse 10 of Luke 13: "Now, He was teaching in one of the synagogues on the Sabbath." Who was? Jesus. He was a teacher. You need to know you need to get that in your spirit. What did He teach? Matthew 8:19, "He was a teacher of the law. He made disciples." You can see this in Mark 4:38. He taught Nicodemus. He wasn't just a teacher in the pulpit; He was a teacher one-on-one. This is one of my main concerns about Fivefold ministries that have become celebrity Christians—they can do things in pulpits they don't live out in their everyday lives.

I love to hang out with people who are the same on and off the platform. If they talk about winning souls, you'll find them out in the week doing just that. You'll find them teaching people. Jesus, when He was on His way to the next place, was teaching Nicodemus. Jesus was going to a tax collector's house and winning souls. He was the real deal. The greatest compliment I've ever received is when someone says to me, "You're real.

14: The Teacher's Porch

You're the real deal." Compliments like, "Man, you've got a great word or man you sure can prophesy," are nice, except when someone says, "You're real," that's what matters most. That's what we need to be at the end of the day. If we are a teacher, then we can't just be a teacher when we turn the gift on during Sunday service. Who are you discipling on Monday, Tuesday, Wednesday, Thursday, and Friday? "Well, I don't have any place to teach. Nobody's given me a pulpit." Build your own! Teach at your coffee table.

The first mention of teacher in the Word of God is found in Psalm 119:99: "I have more understanding than all my teachers, for Your testimonies are my meditation." Wow, that's the first mention of "teacher" in the Bible. And how did he get to that place? By meditating, spending time on the Word, and spending time in His presence.

The church is the primary place where teachers are called to be. They are not called just to be in external schools or universities. Did you know that our schools used to be in the church? Remember "Little House on the Prairie"? The church became the schoolhouse during the week. I believe that needs to happen again. I think this is how we'll shift a generation — when we begin to take responsibility and train them in the way they should go. The proper place for teachers is in the church. I'm not just talking about teachers for school; I'm talking about raising people up in their callings. You see this in Acts 13: the teachers were in Antioch. It mentions the teachers and the prophets. They were there, fasting and praying, and they continued in that "circle of intensity," as the Message Bible says. And from that circle of intensity, of obedience and prayer, they sent forth the apostle Paul and Barnabas.

> *And God hath set some in the church, first apostles, secondarily prophets, thirdly teachers, after that miracles, then gifts of healings, helps, governments, diversities of tongues. 1 Corinthians 12:28 KJV*

Who did He set in the church? Teachers. Where did He set them? Third. Why did He put them third? Because there's an order. It says, "after that, miracles." Why do we not see as many miracles in the church today? Because we've got the order wrong in the church. First Apostles — what does "first" mean? "Proton" — it's the Greek word. The Greek word "proton" means "first" or "chief." Secondarily, prophets. Third, teachers. We need the apostles to decree a thing. We need the prophets to declare a thing. And we need the teachers to explain the thing. We need the Apostolic Doctrine and Prophetic Declarations explained so that we can grow in Kingdom maturity and authority.

Functions of a teacher

We find this in Ephesians 4. Edification. It's beyond facts; it's an impartation of spiritual truth that's illuminated in Scripture by the Holy Spirit. You see this in 1 Corinthians 2:10. It's for our equipping. So, exegesis and hermeneutics are helpful, but Teachers must be taught to rely on the Holy Spirit. Teachers instill a love for the truth and compel believers to go deeper for themselves. Have you ever been around a teacher, and were like, "Man, I never saw that. Man, why didn't I see that? And it provokes you to go and search the Scriptures for yourself. You're like, "Man, how did I miss that?" Have you ever done that? "Holy Spirit, teach me."

The best way to read the Word is like this: You read a verse or so, and then you pray in tongues. Because the letter kills, but the Spirit gives life. So, you read the Word, and then you pray in tongues. When you pray in tongues, you're building up yourself in your most holy faith, but it's also your digestive tract. It's how you digest what you've just read and get it into your spirit man. Then you can move forward. That's why too many people are choking on the Word — they are not digesting it properly. So, you read, and you pray in the Spirit. Read and pray in the Spirit. And then what happens? You go deeper and deeper.

False Teachers

But there were also false prophets among the people, even as there will be false teachers among you, who will secretly bring in destructive heresies,

14: The Teacher's Porch

even denying the Lord who bought them, and bring on themselves swift destruction. 2 Peter 2:1

In 2 Peter 2:1, He's warning us of false prophets and false teachers. They secretly bring in destructive heresies, even denying the Lord. I'm not going to stay here long, but let me just say this: Lately, with social media, anybody who gets a following and a platform seems to become an apostle, prophet, teacher overnight. I do believe God can raise up anyone whenever and however He so desires. However we must be very sober and vigilant who and what we receive into our spirits. Because there are people who will teach and be just a smidge off, and some will not realize it. Just as it is with navigating a ship or airplane if you get one degree off course you will end up miles away from your destination.

Just because they have followers, doesn't mean you should be one!

I don't say this out of fear; I say it with the discerning of spirits. Take time and be cautious. There are people whom I respected in my lifetime who now believe there are more ways to heaven than through Jesus. They once taught, held conferences, and ministered in this nation, and now they're preaching in what they call a church — a congregation that affirms homosexuality. They are now preaching doctrines of inclusion, claiming we are already saved; we just don't know it. These individuals have been led astray and are leading thousands down the same path. There are teachers who were once highly regarded and respected, who, in the last decade have denounced many true teachings. They're leading masses away from the truth of God's Word, and if they don't repent the fall of these leaders and their ministries will be great because they are straying from Scripture.

How to Discern the Counterfeit?

So, I beg you in the name of the Lord, ask the Lord for Wisdom and discernment. How do you know the difference between the true and the false? Spend time with the Truth. If you want to know what's counterfeit, spend time with the real thing. Spend time with the Teacher, with Jesus. Spend time with the Holy Spirit. He will lead you and guide you into all truth. Listen to true teachers who have not moved away from the gospel. Learn from them, and when you hear something that isn't right, your spirit will alert you immediately. As soon as you sense that counterfeit message, you'll recognize it.

Receive the true teachers!

Let's receive the true teachers God is sending forth today, so we can grow in the spirit and are able to teach others also. This will lead the church from just bringing in converts to developing disciples. Churches will become discipleSHIPS who disciple many cities and nations for the Glory of God!

Declaration: "We declare and decree we receive the ministry gift of the Teachers. We will go to the Teacher's Porch and grow in the truth of God's Word. Because we receive the Teachers anointing we will walk in maturity. We will walk and live in your truth, and we will see many others set free because of the truth. In Jesus' name, Amen."

15

Fivefold Leaders, Believers & Centers

How can we raise up Fivefold believers? As we unite and work together as Fivefold leaders we will give birth to Fivefold believers. In order for this to happen, we as Fivefold leaders recognize and receive one another. I don't want to take away your identity as an apostle, prophet, evangelist, pastor or a teacher. I want you to see you need all of the Fivefold. Then together we will be able to develop believers in the fullness of Christ. Jesus said, "I ascended." Why did He descend and ascend? So, that He can fill all things.

We must recognize that He purposely made the body interdependent. We must also recognize others that are apostles, prophets, evangelists, pastors, teachers and partner with them. We must work with them and recognize they're just as necessary. Just as someone will not go to a Brain Surgeon for a foot surgery, we must recognize and receive the grace of each of these ministries. We would never allow somebody who operates on bones to operate on our eyes. We must recognize the necessity of all five and partner with each of them, so we can come into the fulness of Christ.

What if the evangelist goes out as an ox and the church shows the face of an ox? What if the whole church, right face? In a sermon illustration, I line up some people like soldiers and I say either right-face or an about-face and the face of the church shifts from the Lion aka the apostle to the the Eagle aka the prophet or from the Man aka the pastor and the teacher to the Ox aka the evangelist. In this season the face of the Ox is being emphasized. If we're all united with the face of the Ox, functioning in the same grace we will win cities and nations for Christ. When the rest of the Fivefold and church stop saying, "that's not my grace or I don't want to go do evangelism", we will reap the greatest harvest of souls, through the Evangelist's Porch!

These Fivefold shifts might happen monthly, quarterly or annually. However the Holy Spirit leads a particular church or region is what is important. Then if we will, "right face" Shift from the face of the Ox into the face of the man aka pastor. Then the whole congregation moves together in a nurturing anointing. Together we will reveal the heart of the Good Shepherd on the Pastor's Porch. We love and care for them. What if all the prophets become pastoral in that season and love them pastorally? What if all the teaching gifts and all the ministry gifts begin to function with the heart of a shepherd for the flock. Then what happens if we right-faced again and shift? Then we lead then to the Teacher's Porch where we intentionally disciple and ground them in the truth of God's word.

The Bible says, elders should be apt to teach. So, if you're an elder, or a prophet, apostle, evangelist, pastor, teacher, you should shift into the teaching anointing of Christ. This happens on the Teacher's Porch, where believers are equipped and thoroughly furnished in the Gospel. Once you know the truth of God's Word, we shift again and bring you to the Prophet's Porch where you learn to hear the Voice of God, discover your gifts and mature in the prophetic.

Then the prophets usher the people onto the apostle's porch and the apostles say, now you have been won to the Lord. You've been nurtured. Your soul is healed. You've been taught. You've found out who you are. Then the apostles begin to shore you up in your sonship identity. You're not just a servant, you are a son. You realize you are an heir and a joint heir. Then you're commissioned, you're sent, from all five porches.

Colonnade is another word for porch. A colonnade is a walkway. These walkways are Divine runways that we're launched from! When we as believers are raised up on all Five Porches, we will become mature and walk in the fulness of Christ. The greater Glory we've been believing for, will be revealed in and through us. For we will be commissioned and sent forth with the anointing of all of the Fivefold. This will only take place as we move beyond limited, gift centric ministries such as evangelistic centers, teaching centers, prophetic centers, pastoral centers or even apostolic centers and unite as fully functioning Fivefold Centers. I can see this happening locally within congregations, as well as regionally with Fivefold leaders and churches partnering together for the harvest.

Declare this with me

"I declare and decree that The Five Porches are being restored, received and established throughout the church globally today. Fivefold Leaders, Believers and Centers are multiplying exponentially in the nations in Jesus name. I declare and decree that I am a Fivefold believer. I walk, live, and flow in the Fivefold. I receive the grace, the gift, and the anointing of the apostle, and I flow apostolically. I receive grace, the gift, and the anointing of the prophet, and I flow prophetically. I receive the grace, the gift, and the anointing of the evangelist, and I flow evangelistically. I receive the grace, the gift, and the anointing of the pastor, and I flow pastorally. I receive the grace, the gift, and the anointing of the teacher, and I flow in the teaching anointing. Therefore, I am becoming mature in the ways of the Lord. As I flow and operate in maturity, many people will be saved, set free, and established in your Ecclesia. The Greatest Glory and Harvest of all times is coming forth in this hour. To you be all the glory, all the honor, and all the praise. In Jesus' name, Amen."

Joshua Fowler

16

Clear Vision

Where there is no vision the people perish: Proverbs 29:18a KJV

When I entered my 40s, some people said, "you may start to need glasses." I didn't want to receive that! And I didn't at first. At the age of 40, 41, 42, 43, 44, 45, 46, 47, then suddenly, age 48 came, and I needed glasses. I had to go to the optometrist. "Click, click." Then the optometrist says, "How do you see now? Which one is better? Number one or number two?" This is how most of the body has been looking at Jesus. We have looked at ourselves through one lens, maybe two, maybe three, but this is what I see happening. "Click. Click. Click. Click. Click." Now, we will see through all 5 lenses. Now, we will see Christ the way we need to see Him. Now, we will see the Word the way we need to see the Word. Beyond that, we are going to see ourselves through all five lenses that Christ gave.

Remove the Lid!

As I shared earlier, my life was changed as just a 16-year-old kid when The Lord took me up into the heavens and showed me a spirit-filled aircraft carrier with the 5 planes. This encounter is why I began studying the Fivefold ministries over 37 years ago. In this encounter Jesus said, these planes are my Fivefold ministries, study them, gather them together and send them forth. So, after all these years I thought I understood the Fivefold. Having followed The Lord's leadership to hold over 32 Fivefold Roundtables in various cities and nations, one would think I had a grasp of the subject. At the Lord's direction I hosted over 1,500 leaders from 26 nations and 25 states on 05-05-2005 and called it 5-5-5 Global Gathering of Fivefold Leaders. You would think I received the full download. However, over these last few years the Lord has downloaded so much more into me. I imagine that there is still a lot more before the download will be complete. I must repent for teaching from my limited perspective over the last 30 plus years that God is looking for an apostolic center. I think if we call the church an apostolic center then we are limiting His house. This will limit the church to being only one dimensional and only graced apostolically. Everything will be about commissioning and sending and fathering. That's just one dimension of Christ, it's not all five. If we call it a prophetic center, then we're going to want to identify everybody's gifts, prophesy over them and leave them there. A pastoral center, we're going to nurture them, care for them like a shepherd, love them. But they might not have anybody that will prophetically get in their face and tell like it is or an apostle that will help send them out.

We can no longer meet every week and just keep singing, "Just as I am" and just preaching salvation messages. If we do so, after a while, we will have overgrown, 40-year-old babies with bottles and pacifiers in their mouths. Yes, Jesus is The Door, however we must usher them into the fulness of The Kingdom of God. This is possible when we have all five porches working together.

Although the term, Apostolic Centers was our best way to describe what many of us were seeing, it is limited. The Lord revealed to me that He has designed His House to have All Five Porches and that it must be a Fivefold Center. All five porches of the Fivefold must be raised up. Some people might say that's just semantics or that's just terminology, but it's not. Because God does not want us to make the apostolic more important than the prophetic or the prophetic more important than the teaching. He does not want us to make the Teaching more important than pastoral or evangelistic. In fact, I believe God is redefining all fivefold gifts now. Now that we have all five lenses in place, we will see things clearly.

Now as believers we will see ourselves and other believers through all Five lenses. Click, click, click, click, click and we'll know when a believer is ready to be set in a position or sent out. Like the 5 love languages. Many have a more pronounced love language, all of us speak and receive one love language more than another. However if you grow in all of the 5 Love languages, you will be able to speak the love language of your spouse or

16: Clear Vision

child more fluently. So it is when we grow in all Five Facets or languages of Christ, we can speak Apostolic, Prophetic, Evangelistic, Pastoral and Teaching. Rather than saying, I'm of Paul and I'm of Apollos. Rather than saying, "I'm apostolic, prophetic or teaching" what if we combine our our distinct graces and flow in harmony as the Fivefold.

What if you become a Fivefold apostle and you flow in the prophetic, evangelistic, pastoral and teaching anointings? Some say, "all apostles are Fivefold." Having been in many of the apostolic camps and spending time with many apostles around the world, I would beg to differ. I've sat with as many as 80 different nations of apostles. I've been on panels and taught or ministered alongside of them. Many apostles think prophets are from the moon. Many apostles either don't know how to function with prophets or are unwilling to do so. This is a problem. I also speak in some major prophetic conferences and have found that there are many prophets who only identify with prophets. Many of them don't know how to function with apostles and other ministry gifts. I minister in some conferences, where there are some teachers who think prophets are spooky and unbalanced.

In order for this to change, we as Fivefold leaders must also see ourselves through all five lenses. You don't have to lose your identity as an apostle, prophet, evangelist, pastor or a teacher to do so. God desires for you to recognize and see your calling through all five lenses. See it with maturity and develop other believers in the fullness of Christ. Jesus said, "I ascended." Why did I descend and ascend? So, that I can fill all things. When I no longer see myself through just the lens of one gift, but through all of the fivefold lenses, I will see myself and others properly. Most importantly, I will see Jesus more clearly.

I believe this will only happen if we come together like the Knights of The Roundtable and unite our swords together in the center. This will give birth to Fivefold Centers where Christ is in the Center with a plurality of leadership in the church. Fivefold Centers will then raise up and send forth Fivefold Believers into the harvest fields of the nations.

God is releasing His Spirit-filled, aircraft carriers in the earth. God is releasing Fivefold ministries like planes off aircraft-carrier decks. Churches are becoming Fivefold centers instead of love boats.

The Lord chose five porches intentionally. David chose five stones prophetically. Jesus fed the 5,000 with five loaves as a foreshadow of what was to come! Why do we need all five? Because this is what it will take for us to be thoroughly equipped, fully mature, Fivefold believers. This is how we will experience sustainable revival personally and corporately, and disciple fully equipped, mature believers. One dimensional and two-dimensional revival has never proven to be sustainable. I prophesy the Fivefold anointing will be released to usher in the next great awakening! Moving together with the Fivefold anointing, as shown through the Word of God, through the five faces, five loaves, five porches, and five stones. We will see the masses fed spiritually and naturally, and many will be healed and mobilized for the glory of God. We will see believers fully equipped to do the work of the ministry. Identities will be discovered, destinies fulfilled. Giants will be brought down in our lives, over cities and nations. Most importantly, the fullness of Christ will be revealed in the earth.

17

Get on The Porch!

So the young son set off for home. From a long distance away, his father saw him coming, dressed as a beggar, and great compassion swelled up in his heart for his son who was returning home. The father raced out to meet him, swept him up in his arms, hugged him dearly, and kissed him over and over with tender love. "Then the son said, 'Father, I was wrong. I have sinned against you. I could never deserve to be called your son. Just let me be " '—The father interrupted and said, 'Son, you're home now!" 'Turning to his servants, the father said, 'Quick, bring me the best robe, my very own robe; I will place it on his shoulders. Bring the ring, the seal of sonship; I will put it on his finger. Bring out the best shoes you can find for my son. For my beloved son was once dead, but now he's alive! Once he was lost, but now he is found! 'And everyone celebrated with overflowing joy. Luke 15:20-24 TPT

Recently, I had a vision of the Father being on a Porch looking for the Prodigal to return. I heard the Lord say tell them to get on the Porch. He went on saying, tell the Papa's and the Mama's to get on the Porch. He showed me this is both natural dad's and mom's and spiritual fathers and mothers. He showed me we must get into a position to receive the sons and daughters returning home. He said these are the Days of the Great Return. To receive the many sons and daughters returning we must get into position. We must get on the Porch and start looking and praying for their return. Many sons and daughters are coming home both naturally and spiritually. The greatest harvest of souls the church has ever reaped is at the threshold of the Porch. Countless Prodigals are coming home.

Can you hear the Father? "Get on the Porch". Get on your Porch and look for your children to return. Be ready with open arms to receive them and receive them as sons and daughters. Can you hear the Father? "Leader, Get on the Porch!" Man your porch! Whether your porch is the Apostle's Porch, The Prophet's Porch, The Evangelist's Porch, The Pastor's Porch, or The Teacher's Porch get on the Porch that He's called you to. He has called you to partner with all Five Porches to become a fully mature Fivefold Believer and to help raise others up.

Child of God, can you hear His voice? Christ is beckoning from the midst of The Five Porches, "Get on the Porch, receive my fulness and help usher My Greater Glory into the earth.

Author Information

Other Books by Dr. Joshua Fowler:
- Access Granted
- I.D. Required
- Governors of Praise
- ABBA
- Prophetic Praise
- Daily Decrees
- Pause in My Presence

*For More Anointed Books, Courses and Upcoming Events by Dr. Joshua Fowler visit **AwakeTheWorld.org***

Join FiveFold Leaders from around the world:

G5 - Global Fivefold

- **Roundtable**
- **Summit**
- **Alliance**

For More Info: Global5fold.com

Schedule Dr. Joshua Fowler to:

- **Speak for your Church or Conference**
- **Lead a Regional Fivefold Roundtable**
- **Teach Fivefold Modules**

Contact Information:
Awake The World, Inc.
PO Box 1833
Lynn Haven, Florida 32444
booking@AwakeTheWorld.org
407-760-8400

Joshua Fowler

Order Your T-Shirts, Books, Awake Coffee & More Today!

Joshua Fowler

Get Your iProphesy Gear & More Today!

AwakeTheWorld.org

For more information regarding distribution, contact
info@advbooks.com

Orlando, Florida, USA
"we bring dreams to life"™
www.advbookstore.com

www.ingramcontent.com/pod-product-compliance
Lightning Source LLC
Chambersburg PA
CBHW070917160426
43193CB00011B/1499